I Was Douglas Adams's Flatmate

Andrew McGibbon is a comedy writer, performer, director and producer who has made comedies for TV and radio starring Harry Shearer, Bob Monkhouse, Rory Bremner, John Bird, John Sessions, Ian McDiarmid, Bill Nighy, Sally Phillips and Phil Cornwell.

᾽s a drummer he has recorded albums with Morrissey *a Hate*, *Bona Drag*, *Kill Uncle*), Peter Gabriel (*Peace ether*), My Bloody Valentine (*Glider*), Bucks Fizz (*New nnings*), Suggs and Chrissie Hynde.

He lives in London.

I Was Douglas Adams's Flatmate

and Other Encounters with Legends

ANDREW McGIBBON

faber and faber

First published in 2011
by Faber and Faber Limited
Bloomsbury House,
74–77 Great Russell Street,
London WC1B 3DA

Typeset by Ian Bahrami
Printed in England by CPI Mackays, Chatham

A CIP record for this book
is available from the British Library

ISBN 978-0-571-25172-8

2 4 6 8 10 9 7 5 3 1

For Tanya

Contents

Preface

I Was Morrissey's Drummer was the first of what was to become a series of programmes broadcast on BBC Radio 4 in 2005, in which one person's unique encounter with a legend by way of factotemry, flatmatery or, in my own case, drummery created an unusual and very personal insight into the famous one, highlighting the ordinary or mundane things about them or their behaviour that demythologised them, removed the air of perpetual misunderstanding surrounding them and provided a view of greatness through the day-to-day minutiae of their lives: sleeping on a friend's sofa when homeless (Douglas Adams); teaching your PA to fish (Ernest Hemingway); ambushing your tailor on his way to church (Johnny Cash); or firing off a round at your lover, having mistaken her for a burglar (Sam Peckinpah). Just the blissfully ordinary things that great people do. I did not set out to provide a comprehensive, objective version of a legend's life – just a glimpse of harmless private moments that reveal so much more.

After the book was commissioned I took the opportunity to wander further afield, interviewing the lawyer who befriended the innocent British Guantánamo detainee Moazzam Begg, Will Carling's physiotherapist while he was England's rugby union captain in the nineties, and the singer who did a turn standing in for Billie Holiday at the Harlem Apollo in the forties. I spoke to one of the few white dancers in Tina Turner's entourage, the hi-fi store owner who managed jazz legend Chet Baker at the end of his tragic life, a man who wrote jokes for Les Dawson, and a man who hired Dudley Moore to play the piano.

If these great encounters achieve anything they provide us with an affecting view of a unique legend. Setting aside what made them great or famous, be it fashion or substantive talent, whether their significance was justified or overblown, or whether 'it should have been me . . .', as Morrissey once sang, the reality is that the factotums featured in this book can all claim to have 'been there', around the great one when something happened. Of course, 'there' is a largely mythological venue, but a single recrudescence of greatness told primarily through one individual's voice makes these 'journeys with greatness' astonishing, bracing stories, freed from the chains of folklore and invention, feeling at once intimate and full of certitude. Because while the legends encountered may have been (and in some cases remain) extraordinary people, they still suffered ailments, drank to excess occasionally, bumped their heads and fell in love. People like us? Not usually. But people – like us? Yes.

I would like to thank Nick Romero for his endless enthusiasm for the interviews, for helping to balance and order the transcripts in the early part of this project and for editing and offering suggestions for my first drafts; Jonathan Ruffle for organising and setting up the interview subjects on my behalf and providing me with his considerable experience and advice in this area; Ian Greaves for his thorough and exhaustive research and for proofing and correcting the second drafts; Sarah Cuddon for her expert suggestions; Trevor Horwood for his gracious help and smart oversight during the copy-editing process; Kate Ward for her production guidance and help; Caroline Raphael for her wholehearted support of the idea, seeing the potential both in the first show and as a returning series; BBC Radio 4 for backing and promoting the shows; and Hannah Griffiths at Faber and Faber for her strong vision and superb guidance during the preparation of this book and to whom I am indebted for first 'hearing' the possibilities.

My appreciation to Mark Kermode, Duncan Lamont, Ali MacGraw and Peter Shade for additional insights, and to Mark Kermode (again), Clive Langer, David Quantick, Andy Rourke, Stephen Street, Suggs and Danton Supple for their contributions to my own encounter.

Most of all, however, I would like to thank my interviewees: John Bassett, Ann Behringer, Jon Canter, 'Bebop' Jim Coleman, Manuel Cuevas, Katy Haber, Valerie Hemingway, David Nobbs, Nick Potter, Annie Ross and Clive Stafford Smith. They may be, in the context of this book, 'factotums' to the great, notorious and legendary, but one thing I quickly established while talking to them is that they are all no less talented or significant than the people they served and have individually achieved much in their own right.

Andrew McGibbon
May 2010

I

I Was Douglas Adams's Flatmate

I was lying drunk in a field in Innsbruck on one occasion
and I had with me a copy of the *Hitchhiker's Guide to Europe*
and it occurred to me as I stared up at the night sky that
somebody ought to write a *Hitchhiker's Guide to the Galaxy*.
I think this was largely because I thought Innsbruck was
dull . . .
    Douglas Adams, BBC Radio interview, 1984

Comedy writer and novelist Jon Canter met Douglas Adams
while they were students at Cambridge University during the
seventies: a dark, unforgiving decade of power cuts and winters of discontent.

In the seventies, students throughout the Western world
were declaring war on the imperialist structures of the ruling
classes and their elitist anti-proletarian colleges full of the sons
of bloated capitalist running dogs. And at university Canter
and Adams argued over who should lead the proud vanguard
of . . . the Footlights, a politburo of talented Cambridge under-
graduates who, with careers as prestigious surgeons, lawyers
and genetic scientists beckoning, chose to spend much of each
semester in costumes and make-up – many later becoming
highly paid household names at the BBC.

At Cambridge Adams, along with many of his contemporaries (Griff Rhys Jones, Clive Anderson) and friends, was a rabid
fan of *Monty Python*, but unlike his more reticent colleagues,
Adams actively sought out its members, and his endeavours
were rewarded when John Cleese granted him an interview

for a student newspaper. Adams later worked for an extensive period with Graham Chapman on various projects, including a putative but unrealised television comedy that was to feature Ringo Starr. Much to the annoyance of his flatmates, he would play tapes of his brainstorming sessions with Chapman at full blast as if, according to one victim, showing off his new-found credibility in a deafening display of vanity. Perhaps like an ambitious young guitarist given the chance to work with Eric Clapton or Johnny Marr, Adams was simultaneously awe-struck and opportunistic, driven to succeed and emulate his heroes. He also came from a public school that numbers a rich selection of very capable, occasionally narcissistic, borderline sociopaths amongst its alumni – as well as some very well-adjusted people, of course.

According to Canter, Adams was determined to meet not only the Pythons but all his heroes, most of whom were musicians, including Paul Simon, Paul McCartney and members of Pink Floyd, with whom he later played guitar onstage on his forty-second birthday.

The intelligently designed Douglas Adams was one of the greatest comic philosophers to have marvelled at and mocked the court of evolution. His style can be identified instantly by the title of his radio series and first paperback – *The Hitch-hiker's Guide to the Galaxy*. That the unquantifiable vastness of the universe could be mapped out and abridged into a travellers' guidebook is both preposterous and banal. It is also a very, very funny idea.

Adams used the best traditions of English nonsense (Lewis Carroll, Spike Milligan, N. F. Simpson, Monty Python), adding joyful fragments of the pantomime rituals of *Doctor Who*, BBC Television's Saturday-evening sci-fi travelogue about a man who – in case you really have been drinking Pan Galactic Gargle Blasters for the last two millennia in the Restaurant at the End of the Universe – is outwardly an Edwardian-styled eccentric doctor/uncle/inventor but really a time traveller, crossing dimensions and temporal barriers in a time machine disguised as a police box. (As if to prove the point, the actors cast in the title role across the fifty years since the series first appeared on British television have become younger and younger with each reincarnation.)

Significantly, at the time he was penning the radio series of *Hitchhiker's Guide to the Galaxy*, Douglas Adams was a script editor on *Doctor Who*. He was also briefly a staff producer in the BBC's Light Entertainment Radio division, producing BBC Radio 4's weekly satirical show *Week Ending*, for which his flatmate Canter also wrote sketches. *The Hitchhiker's Guide to the Galaxy* bears some of the hallmarks of Adams's brush with *Doctor Who*, but Adams makes the scary green monsters say ridiculous or utterly unexpected things – utterances completely at odds with what they are or appear to be.

This is straight out of the Lewis Carroll school of juxtapositional humour as developed by the godfather of Monty Python, the playwright N. F. Simpson, who sharpened the technique of surprising substitution to a point of genius – a startling and bold literary form of chiaroscuro that illuminates an obscure human truth. Adams deploys this comic device many times in *Hitchhiker*. At the very beginning of the book we meet scary green monsters – the Vogons – who announce that Earth's demolition to make way for a hyperspace bypass will begin in two minutes and that there is no point complaining now as the plans have been on display in the council office on Alpha Centauri for the last two years. This is completely ridiculous and deliciously funny because, while it is unexpected, it is not entirely unbelievable. A race of bureaucratic aliens? The concept is not as ludicrous as it first appears.

As Jon reveals, Adams was obsessed with technology and

also with the possibilities of the World Wide Web, which had just started to function in a primitive way while he was at university in the early seventies. Today no part of the internet remains untouched by some aspect of Douglas Adams's prescient wit and absurd creations. Babelfish, a massively successful internet translation tool, is one such example. The babel fish appears in the *Hitchhiker's Guide* as a fish-cum-earpiece which automatically translates the gobbledegook of aliens from all over the galaxy, allowing easy communication between species. An improbable creation? Perhaps, but its namesake is now available as a free-to-use web tool to obtain quick, if sometimes appropriately hilarious, transcriptions from one language into another.

Another vital element contributing to Douglas Adams's seemingly cosmic arrival in the late seventies was that *The Hitchhiker's Guide to the Galaxy,* and the multimedia cascade that followed in its wake, began life as a humble but instantly popular BBC radio comedy. Radio is a very effective way to communicate highly inventive comic ideas cheaply, using sound effects to stimulate listeners' imaginations to create the science-fiction landscape. However, nothing quite like this had been heard on the radio before – or since – and its originality provided a unique starting point for Adams the comic writer, philosopher and futurist.

Jon Canter did eventually become president of the Cambridge Footlights (he went on to a successful career writing comedy for Lenny Henry, Dawn French, Mel Smith, Griff Rhys Jones and Rowan Atkinson as well as writing novels including the excellent *Seeds of Greatness*). More significantly, though, he became Adams's close friend, sharing various accommodations with him through the post-university years, the success of *Hitchhiker* and the difficult writing periods and depressions that followed his friend's meteoric success. Jon was witness to all these states and recalls the entire experience of someone happy to be travelling with great talent while being a talented writer himself. Not easy.

I met Jon at his home in Suffolk.

*

I was a student at Cambridge from 1971 to 1974, the same time as Douglas. I was at Gonville and Caius and he was at St John's; he was reading English, I was reading Law. I remember our first conversation. We were walking across a lawn in Cambridge and he told me his ambition was to be president of Footlights, and I said, 'No! *I* want to be president of Footlights.' 'No, *I* want to be.' And he never forgot this because he said I should have been more ambitious than I later became, less ambitious than I was as a cocky eighteen-year-old. Which is probably true, but he was far more ambitious . . . right from that moment . . . I remember that vividly.

We were both doing sketches for Footlights. Douglas was writing with two other guys called Will Adams and Martin Smith and they did clever, verbal, Pythonesque sketches and Douglas was always in them, and I remember I had this problem with Douglas because when he used to perform, after he said a funny line, his lips would do this funny moue. Bruce Willis used to do it a lot in his early films. He was famous for doing a movement with his lips which told the audience that what he'd said was pretty cool. Douglas used to do that and it used to piss me off. So that was one of the reasons we weren't very close at that point: the moue. Then, later on, we got very pally, but not in that Cambridge environment.

The most striking thing about Douglas, I remember, was how openly ambitious he was. It's hard for people to believe this now but in the early seventies it wasn't cool to have worldly ambition. Douglas really had that. And the first sign was when he came down to London to interview John Cleese for the university newspaper, and we all thought that was so uncool – to be so openly ambitious, to want to meet the great man. Of course, we all wanted to meet John Cleese, but Douglas did it and was an extra on, I think, Monty Python's *Life of Brian* and got friendly with the Pythons because of that initial contact, which sort of launched him, really.

When I think of him now . . . I've just got a puppy now. It's smaller than Douglas and yet it has some of his characteristics, has a kind of openness and eagerness, boyishness . . . takes me back to the first meeting with Douglas and thinking about what kind of character he was. He wasn't repressed. He was unashamed about things like that. He just wanted to meet John Cleese and was going to do it.

He was quite a curious cult figure, not least because of the scale of him: six foot five, incredibly large gestures, looming, giraffe-like gestures. He would loom into you. So, he was literally unmissable and had this clever verbal gift from the start. But I didn't really get Douglas until later, when he was working as a script editor on *Doctor Who*. I understood then what it was that he had which was very unusual – well, it was to me, anyway: he was an Arts student who had real scientific knowledge and depth of interest, so his breadth was greater than other people's, I think. You couldn't tie him down. His thoughts were bigger because of his knowledge of science, physics . . . he could think cosmically.

He was a great reader of sci-fi: Arthur C. Clarke, Kurt Vonnegut in particular. He always had that interest – that was always his mission, he wanted to combine science fiction with comedy in a way that hadn't been done on TV or radio. Vonnegut had done it in literature as a comic writer. That was where Douglas was forward-thinking – no one had really combined that comic sensibility with scientific knowledge and interest and made something new out of it.

We were slightly wary of each other but then came the great fall. He had to leave university, he had to find something to do, and we both struggled and through the struggle we were brought together. I mean, he was just a guy living on the floor of the house in which I was living.

We weren't close friends at university. We became friends later and that was to do with this house we rented in London – in Arlington Avenue, Islington – which is immortalised in *Hitchhiker*. The phone number of that house is in the book as 2 to the power of 267 709, and the phone number there was 226 7709, hilariously. That was a little code for all of us who lived in the house because he used to come and sleep on the floor when he was script-editing *Doctor Who* and when he was working on the radio series of *Hitchhiker*, and that's when we became friends.

Clare Gorst was one of the original residents of the crowded house in Islington. She recalls the tall visitor just down from Cambridge with nowhere to live ...

We were renting a house in Islington. Four of us had just come down from Cambridge: Jonny Brock, Paul Willcox, Jon Canter and Kim Lewison. Douglas appeared one day and asked if he could stay on the sofa. I had absolutely no inkling that he meant *stay* stay. I thought he just wanted a space. He chose it because it was the biggest sofa I'd ever seen – about the only sofa in the world that could fit

Douglas Adams. And he just stayed. In the morning there were always shoes strewn around, shoes big enough to house a rabbit. The space he took up was incredible. He and I used to stay up quite late. He was deeply unhappy at that point. He thought he might have to go and work for a bank in the Far East – Jardine Matheson. To him it seemed like a fate worse than death. When I asked him what he did all day he said he typed on his typewriter. So no one had any inkling of what was going to appear. We never asked what he was writing. I enjoyed his company.

I remember explaining to him that, now that we had jobs, we couldn't have the typewriter going on all night, and he seemed very surprised by that. It perplexed him.

Clare also recalls that long after Douglas left and enjoyed success, they were treated to a bizarre range of unexpected phone calls at the Islington house. In that pre-telesales era when nuisance calls were relatively rare, she found them a pleasing novelty.

People used to ring us up and ask for various characters in the book, especially Marvin, and I always treated them respectfully. I'd say, 'Sorry, I'm afraid Marvin isn't in at the moment.' But they continued after we'd moved out. The person who moved in after us had no idea why he was getting these strange phone calls until one day he was flying to New York and was reading the *Hitchhiker's Guide*. He read the telephone number, the light dawned and he leapt out of his seat shouting, 'Now I understand!'

Jon Canter recalls the chaos of the Islington houseshare before its soon-to-be-infamous phone number became part of *Hitchhiker* folklore.

Five people lived at 29 Arlington Avenue, N1: two couples

and me. One of the couples, Jonny and Clare – spring 1978 – said they were having a baby and the baby needed my room. So at that point it was an impetus to move out; Douglas didn't have anywhere to live, so I took it upon myself to find a flat we could share. Our stomping ground was Highbury. I found a flat, 19 Kingsdown Road, just off Holloway Road, north of the Odeon, and we moved in together in the autumn of 1978. That was where he wrote *Hitchhiker's Guide* . . .

To say we had our own space is a misnomer, because everything in that flat was pinched; he was six foot five, I was six foot two. We could not go into the kitchen side by side. One of us had to go first, followed by the other; if the first in wanted to come out, the other had to withdraw. So it was a very restrictive environment for two oversized youths. It was also fantastically depressing because on the ground floor there was a mustachioed woman, about ninety or ninety-five, who used to have this mantra, saying, 'He's gone, he's gone!' We worked out that this was her husband who'd been killed in the Second World War, or possibly the First, and he was not going to come back. So every time you came into this house, which consisted of three flats, you would have her to deal with because you couldn't get to the stairs without talking to her. So we did the best we could with her. We were on the first floor; above us was a gay Canadian architect – he did a lot of business . . . this was the seventies before things calmed down. So there was this constant passage of people from above us, and there was this tragic and ripe-smelling lady below us – she was just another tenant . . . thankfully she wasn't the landlady – so it was the kind of flat where you wanted to stay indoors, so you wouldn't have any difficult encounters when you went out of the flat. It was a sort of prison.

Douglas was extremely messy, as was I. He was fantastically ramshackle and accident-prone. He had enormous gestures; if you put your hands out three foot in front of you and point the palms of your hands towards your own shoulders, and then move the hands up and down, that's the classic Douglas gesture that accompanied lots of his thoughts. And don't try this at home, because if you do you might knock something over. He did knock things over. Douglas wasn't mad but he was manic, so he would have sudden, huge fits of manic enthusiasm for things, for people, for words, sounds, so that was another cause of his clumsiness to which he was prone; which was great, which was part of that puppyish charm I referred to earlier – this enormous, intellectual, musical excitement, and sexual too. A great man for sex – he taught me.

I would like to pay tribute to him. Maybe because he grew up in the country he had no hang-ups about sex, so he was a cheerful rogerer, whereas I was a neurotic Jewish Woody Allen. Douglas was more like something out of *Lady Chatterley* and I remember that was a real gulf between us. Anyway, the sexual excitement, the intellectual excitement and the fascination with famous people, he had that side, that was a pointer.

He wanted to meet people he liked. That business of interviewing John Cleese – that was very typical. If he liked somebody, he wanted to be part of his or her life.

There's a wonderful anecdote. When he became famous he wanted to meet Paul Simon, who was the musician he most admired. Douglas was a lefty and a very good guitarist, and Paul Simon is a left-handed guitarist. So you had Hendrix, Simon, McCartney [all left-handed], all people he'd like to have met. Anyway, when he became famous, living in New York, he tried to meet Paul Simon, who had heard of Douglas and sent a message via his management saying, 'How tall are you?' And Douglas replied, 'I'm six foot five.' And the message came back that Paul Simon did not want to meet him, and this is the only evidence Douglas had of why not. Did the fact that Paul Simon was a short-arse mean that Douglas was too big to meet him? 'I'm too big to meet you . . . no really, I'm too big!' So that was a disappointment, but he did meet most of the heroes that he had.

He really wanted to meet the Beatles, and Douglas worked on a script with Graham Chapman for Ringo which never happened because there were problems with the script and Ringo doesn't do problems. He met Ringo, he met Paul McCartney. He once came back to the flat and told me he'd been to a party and met a rather shy man, George Harrison. I couldn't help feeling for George Harrison because I imagined what it must have been like being pursued round the room by the giant eager form of Douglas. Then the sting in the tail. I had to break the news to him that John Lennon had died. It was in Douglas's bedroom in Highbury. He was completely dis-traught and probably spent about thirty-six hours in bed, but his friends, who were piss-artists and cynics to a man, could not help observing that John Lennon was the only Beatle Douglas hadn't met, and that one of the sadnesses of John's death was that it deprived Douglas of the chance to meet him.

If things weren't going well for him in his romantic life he was like a wounded beast and would just sit on his own for hours, playing the guitar or listening to the music he loved. Or he would withdraw to the bath; Douglas's baths were legendary, they were so long you think he'd come out and be a sausage. It was remarkable. Then it was a joke; now I would say it was a sign of someone who was unreachable for various periods of his life, of his day.

It was very noticeable. You can't be too straightforward about this, because this is part of what it takes to be a writer. I don't think you can be a writer without being massively self-indulgent. It's almost a definition of what it is. He would be indulging himself in his thoughts. So he was depressed. You could say it was down time, or more likely he was just in there musing, mostly with self-pity but not entirely. He certainly couldn't have written anything without the baths.

I would come home from work to be greeted by this howling banshee sound of Kate Bush singing 'Wuthering Heights'. And, if you remember, this was her first ever record. No one had heard of her before. I think she was sixteen years old and she was astonishing.* Douglas was hooked on this record to such an extent that I don't think he could work without it, so he would play it thirty and forty times and what was so wonderful – almost like a simpleton – was that the record never got less exciting for him. His eyes would light up every time he played it. And he just fell in love with it and it sustained him through the months of writing that book. It was almost as if she had an otherworldly sound to her voice. She was, dare I say it, almost alien in the way she sang and I think he connected with that and it became a voice that took him to the other worlds in his imagination.

Douglas wasn't a great drinker. Drink and drugs were not really what he was about. There was only one incident I remember that was drink-related. In the flat in Highbury after *Hitchhiker* had come out and been a huge success, he suddenly said to me, 'Do you fancy some Coca-Cola?' And

* Although aged sixteen when signed by her record company, Bush was nineteen when 'Wuthering Heights' was released in 1978.

I said, 'No . . . I never fancied it.' And then he said, 'I just think I'll go to the off-licence and get some Coca-Cola.' So off he went, with a curious excited gleam, and when he came back ten minutes later he was carrying two trays of Coca-Cola – there must have been 144 cans of Coca-Cola. It was a remarkable sight – this great man with this giant store of Coca-Cola. And I realised he'd gone into the off-licence and had thought, 'My life is good! I don't have to buy one can of Coca-Cola any more. Off-licence holder, give me all of your Coca Cola!'

But that is a story about excess related to drink that isn't alcoholic.

Douglas had to be the first with all kinds of new technology. He was the first person I ever knew to own a computer. He actually gave me an Apple Mac before anyone knew what an Apple Mac was. I remember it had a Silk Cut burn. I treasured that burn; it was made by Douglas's own Silk Cut. In about 1981 he got himself a cordless phone, not a mobile phone. Remember, you could take the phone off the base and you could wander round with it, and you could see Douglas thinking, 'How am I going to tell the person on the other end that they're talking to me on a cordless phone?' And one day he was in the sitting room talking to a friend and he wandered out of the sitting room and into the bathroom, and then there was the unmistakable sound of a tinkle and it was Douglas thinking, 'The only way I can prove to the person on the other end of the line that I'm mobile is if I wander to the lavatory with the phone and have a wee-wee while I'm talking to them.' It was the most bizarre and unsettling sound. I never saw it but there he was with one hand on the future and one hand on himself, if you like. I mean, it was just so overtly showing off. But that was the thing about him – as I tell this story it seems to me true: the deader he gets, the funnier he gets. I hope that doesn't sound offensive, but it's true. I recall this wonderfully comic side to him where you could see the way he was thinking. He was a man who couldn't resist expressing an idea if he had it, especially if it was an idea where he was ahead of everyone else when it came to technology.

I wasn't part of *Hitchhiker's* creation, although he would tell me of key details that he'd put in that somehow related to me or our common experience. For example, we went on holiday to Corfu and shared a villa and he came in and said, 'I don't know where my towel is.' What kind of person is twenty-six years old and doesn't know where his towel is? And, as you know, that became the iconic object in *Hitchhiker*, and sweetly, when the film [directed by Garth Jennings] came out, at the premiere, they actually issued little towels with the *Hitchhiker* thumb on them. And also he was meticulously fair in crediting me with a line I'd written for a monologue I'd done about a miserable northern git when we were both students. The monologue began, 'Life? Don't talk to me about life!' And Douglas said, 'I want to use that line,' and it became Marvin the Paranoid Android's key line. So he was meticulously fair. He didn't nick stuff. He told you what he was doing.

We both had a love of American sitcom. Douglas in his heart had a great hankering to be American. Towards the end of his life he lived in Santa Barbara and the two things we used to watch endlessly – this is before video, so we had to be there at the time – were *M*A*S*H* and *Soap*. *Soap* was an inspired surreal sitcom based on daytime US soap operas. Neither of these is a work of sci-fi and yet something about the humour . . . Americans famously don't do irony – well, that's nonsense. They are the most ironic people of them all. So, if you think back to the kind of humour that *M*A*S*H* was doing and consider that his book [*Hitchhiker*] began with the end of the world . . . I think *M*A*S*H* had a similar dark heart – it was about the madness of war. I think that did influence him.

I was working as an ad copywriter. Douglas had got famous and rich as a result of *Hitchhiker*, decided to leave the Holloway Road flat and moved to a more sumptuous flat in Highbury New Park, and he said, 'You can have a room in my flat.' That's a shift in the balance. We were joint tenants. Although he didn't say anything it did mark a change.

He was incredibly benevolent, benign.

He did like my company. He regarded all of us [our friends] as causes. He wanted us to achieve what we hadn't. From his vantage point he definitely wanted others to join him scaling the heights. When he produced *Week Ending* [for BBC Radio 4] before *Hitchhiker*, I was one of the first people he rang and he said, 'I want you to write for this, get off your arse.' The *Week Ending* gig was one of the first things I got. I don't think he was a natural producer. I think he just wanted a job. The job he did have was script-editing *Doctor Who*, and that was a real stepping stone. I think it preceded *Hitchhiker*. I think he submitted ideas for the programme and ended up meeting the producers.

Nick Webb at Pan Books suggested turning the radio show into a book, which led to global acclaim.

He was always my friend and never made me feel less because he was famous, but things were different. I remember coming back to the flat to hear Douglas sitting on a sofa talking to a woman in her twenties in a particular way. I had walked into something I shouldn't have walked into. He was being interviewed. It was strange. There are certain tones of voice people have when they're being interviewed.

Also, messages Douglas took for me were mundane but messages I took for Douglas were things like his shoemaker – he did have big feet. Another day, an American producer asked whether Douglas was there. He introduced himself and proceeded to list his credits in the film business, which were considerable. He wanted to make a film of *Hitchhiker*, but he was too far into the pitch to realise that he was talking to the wrong guy. He had started so he was going to finish. I couldn't stop him. Douglas was an industry. Simply by answering the phone you became part of that industry.

At this point he was at his happiest. He'd written the first book, it was a huge success, people loved it and he felt vindicated that he'd done this. I think the depression really kicked in when he had to write his second book. Now, the world was making demands on him – he was obligated to the world. There is a sense of people waiting for you to do your work. He found it unbearable. Although he wrote in the Highbury flat, he had to be imprisoned in the hotel next door to finish it. Two things struck me; how painful that was compared to the joy he had writing the first one; and secondly – and this is a writers' thing – if you're so close to the deadline anything you deliver will be taken – like a bike waiting to take something to the printers – so it's almost a way of forestalling criticism and rewriting. Not a good thing, but that's how it happened. I find it sad to look back on that because Douglas took so much joy in his writing.

I think it was all brilliant but there were times in the later books when I felt he was tap dancing – producing stuff. If you're not quite clear where the story's going you'll spend time describing where you are so you don't have to think about moving forward. That characterises his later work. Sentence by sentence it's brilliant but there isn't the overarching thing to put you forward. Also, Douglas had so many things in his life. He was a philosopher of technology. He was unconservative, ahead of the game, had a love of computers; this is why he became a Californian, not hidebound.

The place was bigger. We didn't look after it well. Lots of take-away food. [Comedy writer] John Lloyd called me and Douglas Desperate Dan, saying we turned everything we ate into cow pie and our giant mouths never closed properly.

Douglas's obsession with music became total at that point. He kept buying guitars. He was a gifted guitarist and also there's nothing better for a writer than a displacement activity like playing a musical instrument. The more money he got, the more guitars he got in.

Famously, he played on his forty-second birthday. Met the Floyd and played with them at Wembley. He worshipped musicians.

I don't think Douglas was that concerned with his environment. It was a burden to have to buy a big house and have to fill it. Luckily, he got in with two architects – Richard Paxton and Heidi Locher – of the minimalist persuasion, so he didn't have to fill his rooms with stuff. He built a temple in his house in Islington after we shared a flat and created a 'guitar-henge', and you had to enter quietly. So if you were talking about furnishings, then upright guitars in stands and a grand piano were the things he really loved.

His affairs were cosmic love affairs destined to end as fireballs and burn out; shooting stars or something. So, no, not protracted, but they were intense. He got romantically wounded and would have to play seventeen sides of Paul Simon to recover from romantic setbacks.

None of our flatshare friends were connected with show business, but he was loyal to them. The thing about Douglas was that he couldn't hide his obsessions. One evening I made some pasta, seven or eight times more than was needed for Paul and Clare [Gorst], who were two friends who'd lived with me in Islington before Douglas. About halfway through the pasta course Douglas suddenly took it upon himself to illustrate the greatness of Ringo Starr's drumming at volume eleven. They were baffled but this was one of his great causes – Ringo's drumming. At that point in the history of pop I don't think people thought of Ringo as a good drummer anyway, but for the next hour dinner was suspended as Douglas took us through the Beatles, complete with fills.

He was like a mad professor. Another comedy trait of Douglas's was his creation of epithets and similes. Here's an example. Douglas might say that watching Elvis Costello was rather like wrestling an elephant. Take it on trust that it was. Douglas having come up with this image, he would tell you and then look rather excited and nervous like a bird of prey. He'd be looking for someone to pounce on. He'd phone eighteen of our friends, ask them how they were and then run the epithet past them. Nothing got wasted.

I think he may have married Jane because of an epithet: 'We tried everything else so we thought we'd try marriage.'* 'Douglas, I know why you've got married and the only way you can use it is at a wedding reception.' There was love but also that line.

Douglas had no interest in sport. If you are into sport, you play it and it occupies a serious part of your mind – you're going to spend large portions of your day thinking about sport. All day I dream about sport. In Douglas's case, that

* Adams married barrister Jane Belson in 1991. They had one daughter.

whole cerebral area could be taken up with proper thoughts about stuff whereas for the rest of us we're thinking, 'I wonder if Andy Murray's going to win the US Open?' So it was wonderful to watch him doing any kind of football. It was like watching a stag trying to play football, this huge frame on these shaky knees; it was terrible but also lucky for him.

He was a terrible driver. He had a manic attitude to gear changes, second, third, fourth, what was going on. It didn't seem to relate to what was happening on the road. He just got excited by the prospect that he could change gear. I don't recall any crashes, but if you had to plump for a way Douglas might go, he might well have gone for a bit of a smash.

I left the flat in 1981. No reason, really. Douglas wanted to move into another flat in Islington and I felt the time had come. But the friendship was very secure. We only drifted apart when I moved to Suffolk and he moved to California. I moved to Stoke Newington after Highbury with the writer Sue Limb.

In my home here in Suffolk a mutual friend, Mary Allen, rang to say he'd died. He'd had a heart attack from over-exercise.* My sadness is that the last years of his life hadn't borne the fruit, i.e. a film of *Hitchhiker*. He spent a long-time on the screenplay. He had been fired, the producers got in someone who wrote like Douglas, and when that didn't work out they thought it best to get in Douglas to do Douglas. Director Jay Roach [who directed the Austin Powers films] was going to make it, then it didn't happen. And then Douglas died before the film was ever made, so that was really sad – all his energies that weren't going into lectures were going into the screenplay. The lecture circuit fired him towards the end of his life. He was hailed as a guru. He got standing ovations at Mac conferences and he

---

* Adams died in May 2001, aged forty-nine.

could go back to being a performer. So towards the end of his life he felt very fulfilled by being onstage.

I've got two books by Douglas, *The Long Dark Tea-Time of the Soul* and *Dirk Gently*, and they both have the same dedication:

Fuck off Jon, Douglas!

There is a reason for this. Douglas and I used to say if you knew an author, the only way you could prove it was if he gave you an autograph in a book. He had to put something personal and there was nothing more personal than 'fuck off' because he will only say that to someone he knows well. So that's something I treasure as I can hear him saying it with such affection!

Douglas and I had a party trick. I could sing 'The Boxer' with Douglas playing guitar. In Corfu we used to sing this, but my harmonies were not good. We always did this late at night. He loved that acoustic finger-picking Paul Simon style. We also loved watching and listening to the sound-track of *The Last Waltz*. It was a key film when Douglas and I shared a flat. It had so many of the people we loved in it.

In the flat in Holloway Road we had a sitting room that was maybe ten foot by six. My most precious souvenir of Douglas is a photo taken in one corner of that room by the window. I'm standing in front of a poster of Van Gogh's *Blue Irises*. I've got round John Lennon glasses, a kind of gay, Californian cop moustache and a very hideous paisley patterned sweater that my sister brought me from the Bologna book festival. Douglas is looking up at me; he's wearing a brown leather jacket. That's the one he really loved. He's got a very fine head of dark hair; he's got a cigarette, which would be a Rothmans, and he's just looking up at me with affection, and it's just delightful.

I Was Chet Baker's Final
Tour Manager

My mother went into the bathroom after Chet, and she came out yelling someone had just burned rope in the bathroom. People on Long Island in the fifties didn't know much about marijuana . . .

In the thirties and forties, morphine (a man-made synthesis of opium which, like laudanum, was intended to help opium addicts overcome their dependency) was replaced by bubbling mustard, a sugar-like heroin form, designed originally to get people off the preceding three. Heroin abuse ushered in a whole new fashion of drug addiction which, in combination with a contiguous rise in the smoking of cannabis and weed, created a new soft-celled, womb-like happy place where judgemental parents and elders, screaming government hysteria and your skin colour or background didn't matter. Heroin use became particularly attractive to artists and was especially popular amongst jazz musicians. Almost a badge of honour, it could also be a destructive part of their artistic journey.

Chet Baker, a jazz trumpeter and singer, was also a heroin addict. He joined the US army at sixteen and was posted to Berlin – a city then split into four zones each run by a different Allied occupier following the Second World War. He had joined the army to play music, because being a musician in the army meant that he could practise all day instead of becoming a bored GI, mashed up on grain whiskey, picking off mockingbirds in prickly-pear bushes behind the shooting range.

Pursuing music rather than bird watching, Chet left the army after two years to study theory and harmony at El Camino College, dropping out of college to join up again, this time with the Sixth Army band at the Presidio in San Francisco.

In the evenings he would sit in alongside musicians at jazz clubs and play. Eventually he was to link up with saxophonists Stan Getz (arrested after trying to rob a pharmacy to get a fix of morphine described by one fellow player as 'a nice bunch of guys') and most significantly with Charlie Parker (started on morphine as pain relief after a bad car accident, which led to an addiction to heroin), who toured with him on the West Coast. When he joined the Gerry Mulligan (heroin addiction; prison time for it) quartet in 1952, he became a phenomenon, at the heart of the world's first pianoless jazz quartet and the originator of cool jazz. Using their instruments – Mulligan on baritone sax and Baker on trumpet and vocals – in engaging, contrapuntal improvisations that whispered modal structures rather than exposing the vacuum of missing piano chords, and accompanied by only a bass player and drummer (respectively, Bob Whitlock and Chico Hamilton, brother to Bernie Hamilton, the permanently harried police chief, Harold Dobey, in *Starsky and Hutch*), they made a startling breakthrough. Chet Baker, the singing, trumpet-playing virtuoso was hatched.

As subversive as Elvis to the parents of the bobbysoxed youngsters left behind in Oklahoma during the war, cool jazz was evolving into a dissident fashion for the older, mature, seen-a-bit-of-action-in-Italy set. But it wasn't long before it too flowed into the mainstream to become the musical language of fifties white America. When the elements of sex, jazz and cool combined they created the equivalent of an intellectual nuclear fusion. Nothing encapsulates that explosion better than the arrival on the jazz scene of Chet Baker.

A man with Okie blood in his veins, Chet, played the trumpet with a unique, melancholic tone. He also sang with an almost ethereal timbre that poured beauty, youth and musical wonder into the ears of jazz addicts everywhere. In looks, he was an Elvis Presley for the jazz world. Chet's cool, brilliant trumpet playing, pushing the boundaries of his inspiring hero Miles Davis even further, and his charming, good-looking white-boy-next-door image helped to ease hardened American audiences away from the feeling that jazz was a musical idiom created by reefer-smoking, vein-munching, needle-hound beatnik weirdos and their sidekicks from the ghetto into something that the Nussenbaums from White Plains, NY, might enjoy listening to on an LP.

Chet's heroin addiction brought with it all the horrors and disgraces that come with having a 'monkey on your back', but it wasn't heroin that killed him.

I travelled to New York to meet 'Bebop' Jim Coleman, owner of the excellent and very accommodating high-end AV equipment store Audio-Video Salon on 2nd Avenue. Jim managed Chet's touring schedules for the last four years of his life. Chet, criminalised by heroin addiction, was banned from playing in certain American clubs. He had been busted in Europe too.

Jim and Chet's friendship stretched all the way back to high school.

*

I met Chet Baker when I was thirteen years old. My cousin Jeanie married Chet's first bass player, Carson Smith, and they were all located in Los Angeles, California.

I've always felt that the term 'West Coast jazz' was sort of a code for saying 'white jazz'. When you think of the guys that founded this type of movement, Shorty Rogers would probably be the first. He was a good swing trumpet player, originally from New York, and played with the Woody

Herman band. He ended up in California arranging and composing, and played with Stan Kenton too. And he sort of got that thing going, a very light feeling in the rhythm section. There were some black guys in the music too.

They basically played standards. I think they were trying to emulate the way Miles Davis was playing in the early fifties. Miles changed his way of playing when he was on the Prestige label, where he was just playing standards. I don't think he knew standards as well as he had known jazz original songs, but it was very popular and everybody tried to emulate that, including Chet Baker. Chet knew the songs better than Miles, and eventually it evolved to the point where Chet was actually more involved harmonically with the music.

Chet Baker burst on the scene in 1954. He had actually played the trumpet in the army band for many years before that. He went into the army band in 1946. I think he did three or four years, and then he went back and did another two or three years. What happens when you're in the army band, or any military band, is you practise eight hours a day. So he had tremendous chops, and he really could play. Plus, when he was a kid, his mother took him to talent shows and he sang standards. So when you take into consideration that Chet is not only playing a song like Miles Davis did, but also knew the lyrics of the song and got a better feeling for what the author of the song intended . . . I think that helped him a lot in what he did.

The other thing is, of course, that like many of his age and his ilk, he was totally, totally fascinated by Charlie Parker and the bebop movement. Charlie Parker came to LA in 1951 to play, and he put out a call for a trumpet player. Every jazz trumpet player in LA showed up. What Chet Baker did, which is amazing – some people say Chet was from another planet, and this might prove it – Charlie Parker played a solo, and then Chet played the same solo, which is mind-boggling. Charlie Parker caught it right away, and said, 'This guy is the guy for me.' He realised that Chet was so far advanced in terms of thinking in the abstract and actually creating and improvising.

Chet wasn't known as a great reader of music. He didn't come from the big bands like all his contemporaries did. He played in the army band, he sang, he listened to Charlie Parker records like everybody else, and he played jazz. He was strictly a musician, strictly into jazz, but he's almost like a folk legend or a folk hero, because of what he did. He was a good-looking guy too when he was younger.

Chet became an overnight sensation after he recorded with Gerry Mulligan in 1954, and Pacific Jazz also recorded him separately. This is, of course, when they did some of the classic standards such as 'My Funny Valentine'. Gerry Mulligan was a very interesting guy and had come up in the forties arranging for big bands such as Claude Thornhill's Band and the Gene Krupa Band. He was a good baritone sax player as well, and he had a habit. Chet hooked up with him in the early fifties – they played sporadically together throughout their careers – but they didn't get along well. I think Gerry Mulligan had a very big ego and so did Chet.

In the early fifties, what Chet Baker was doing in California was what most people did. He smoked cigarettes like everybody else, did a lot of surfing, and he probably smoked some marijuana, some weed. It was when he went on his first tour of Europe [in 1955] that he got hooked up with some people like Dick Twardzik, the great pianist who OD'd and died on that tour. I think this is when Chet started to use heroin. He had a tremendous reputation at this point; he'd won the *Down Beat* poll several times in a row, the new star poll. I think he was tired of California.

The *Today* show, which is still on the air on NBC Television in the United States, was hosted at the time by a guy named Dave Garroway, and he was a big jazz fan. He invited Chet Baker and his quartet to come to New York, and Chet got an engagement at Birdland, on 51st Street and Broadway, which was the jazz capital of the world back in the fifties. Now it's a topless club called Flashdancers, but it's still there. Jazz pilgrims can still go down the same steps that Chet Baker went down in the fifties and check Flashdancers out.

Chet and his band stayed at my house on Long Island. I remember one very interesting incident at that point. My mother went into the bathroom after Chet, and she came out yelling someone had just burned rope in the bathroom. [*Laughs*] People on Long Island in the fifties didn't know much about marijuana, and that was her first meeting with Chet Baker.

Basically in the late fifties he hung out in New York. I think he really got into the drug scene, and he wanted those hotter New York rhythm sections. People come to New York because of the great rhythm sections: the great pianists, bass players and drummers. Orrin Keepnews, one of the great jazz producers of all time, signed Chet up on his Riverside label. There were some very good recordings done in New York with Chet Baker in the late fifties.

Then our paths sort of coincided. In 1960 I got a scholarship to study at the Conservatory of Santa Cecilia in Rome – I played the trumpet – and coincidentally Chet was based in Italy in 1960. Unfortunately, this was when he was arrested. The Italian government and the Italians didn't mind exporting heroin all over the world, but they didn't want anybody using it in their country.

Some detectives followed Chet around until they finally caught him going into a gas station men's room and shooting up. For this he got eighteen months in a psychiatric ward. It also blemished his entire reputation in Europe. He really couldn't stay anywhere in Europe after this happened. Chet also had some problems in the UK. I think they locked him up there as well.

Peter Cook once wrote an article about how in 1963 the Home Secretary prevented Lenny Bruce from entering the country to perform at Cook's club, the Establishment, on the grounds of his heroin conviction. For Chet, the drug convictions became the equivalent of prison tattoos. Even if you have them burned off you can still see the marks of the incarceration complex and the authorities never forget – especially if you're famous.

At the same time, he married a woman named Carol, and to this day she is known as Chet Baker's widow. She was a dancer in Rome. Chet ended up back in the United States, I would say probably 1963, 1964. He was originally from Oklahoma, although his parents had moved from Oklahoma to California when he was a young kid. He took Carol, and I think they had several young children at the time, to live in Yale, Oklahoma. She was a very dutiful wife. I think she let it really slide over her head to what extent Chet was using drugs.

We also had problems in New York. We had what are known as the cabaret laws. This is a law that would not allow anybody who had a police record of any kind to work in any establishment that had a liquor licence. This stopped Billie Holiday from working in Manhattan. She worked at the club my mother managed out on Long Island, the Cork and Bib, until she died in 1959. Art Blakey couldn't work in

New York; Chet Baker couldn't work in Manhattan, or any of the five boroughs for that matter, so it was a very difficult situation.

So Chet did come back to the States, and ironically the first place he worked when he came back to New York in the sixties was the Cork and Bib, because he could work there legally. Then he went out to the coast because he was comfortable out there: he'd lived in California for years, and he tried to get involved in so many different things. Someone came up with the idea of him copying Herb Alpert and the Tijuana Brass. I think it was Chet Baker and the Mariachi Brass, you know, things along those lines. He had a wife then and some children and he tried very hard to support them, but it didn't work. It wasn't that easy at that point. The dew was off the lily; his image was tarnished. I always thought that if you were a black guy and you used heroin, it might help you a little bit with your public relations. If you're a white guy in the United States in the fifties and sixties, and you used heroin, forget it. You were blackballed. And that's basically what happened to Chet.

But it's interesting – he really had focus, and the focus was on being a better improviser and a better musician. He never really thought of, like, Freddie Hubbard, going commercial and making bubblegum jazz. He wanted to pursue the path that Miles Davis had started. And even though Miles got off that path in the late sixties and early seventies to make money, and become more successful on a material and popular plane, Chet never did that. He would continue to go from city to city, country to country, and play straight-ahead jazz. Sometimes with broken-down trumpets, and most of the time with broken-down rhythm sections, but it never stopped him.

Chet tried very hard to make a living playing the trumpet. It was difficult. Very difficult, considering that he had a full-fledged heroin addiction while being married and having kids. He ran up a tab with some drug dealers in San Francisco and unfortunately they felt the best way to retaliate against someone who doesn't pay their bills is, in terms of trumpet players, knock their teeth out. And they knocked Chet's teeth out; he just said he was mugged, but this is the basic consensus of what happened.

So then he got menial jobs, such as pumping gas, and he tried to make it. A few years later he went back to practising the trumpet, and it probably took him a good three or four years of practising without a full set of teeth: there is a certain amount of pressure that is needed for the embouchure to work. Chet was famous for borrowing trumpets wherever he went but he always used the same mouthpiece. He redeveloped an embouchure without teeth. There was a dentist in Texas that had been working on various bridges and things, and Chet at certain points had more teeth than other times. In other words, he would have something he could slide in over his gums that would work like teeth. But he never really had teeth from 1967 until he passed.

Jim's and Chet's lives continued to interweave.

Dizzy Gillespie got him a job at a jazz club on West 53rd Street called the Half Note. The original Half Note had been down on Hudson Street in the village, run by the Cantonero family, really nice people, and for some reason they decided to move into Midtown – they thought they would get some more tourist action, I guess, and it was a very unsuccessful thing. But they lasted a few years on 53rd Street, between 6th and 7th Avenue, around the corner from the Hilton Hotel. It became a topless bar after that.

So Dizzy Gillespie got Chet a job there, and Chet came

from California, bringing his family with him. I'm standing in front of my store one day – I've been here since 1969
– and Chet Baker walks by. So remember, I'd met him in
1954. And then I saw him in 1960 in Italy. And then there
he was in 1973.

I play the trumpet, and I still play the trumpet to this
day, but obviously I don't get a chance to play it much
because I'm here all the time working. I got married in 1969
and I had to stop playing the trumpet full time because my
wife didn't want me to have any fun. We have live music
workshops here, and a lot of the great jazz trumpet players
in New York still hang out here and play. So I opened this
business, and I'm standing outside and Chet Baker walks
by. I say, 'Hey? What are you doing here?'

He said, 'Oh, living in New York now.' He was living at
Rupert Towers at 90th and 3rd Avenue.

There was a jazz club on 86th Street, between Central
Park West and Columbus, called Strikers, and Lee Konitz
was working there. Lee Konitz still lives on 86th Street. We
still see him around – eighty-something years old! Chet and
Lee Konitz played at Strikers all the time.

I was busy over here, and I didn't get over there too
much. In 1978, Charlie Haden the bass player would come
in here, and I remember he took me to his apartment on
the West Side. He opened the refrigerator and said, 'That's
my methadone and that's Chet's methadone.' So he would
keep Chet's methadone in the refrigerator for him.

Then Chet left New York again and basically lived in
Europe. The drug ban was off and he was accepted. He
did much better in Europe than he did here. He lived in
Holland a lot and he could always get drugs there; I think it
helped him. He could also make much more money touring Europe than he could in the United States.

In the fifties there might have been forty jazz clubs in the United States, and you could do a real tour. Today, if there are seven or eight jazz clubs in the United States, I'd be amazed. Maybe one club in LA, one club in Detroit, one in Chicago, one in San Francisco, one in Seattle, Washington, maybe New Orleans, Philadelphia. Not much happening.

At any rate, Chet would come back to the United States because his family, his wife and three kids still lived in Yale, Oklahoma, believe it or not. They were still waiting for him to come back and his mother was there. He would stop by and see them every year or two; he would go to LA and get some work out there. He also set things up so that wherever he went he would have connections to buy heroin. He had a very good drummer named Leo Mitchell who was his friend here in New York, and Leo was always helping him.

Chet was able to fill a jazz club in Manhattan twice a year and get top dollar. It's the same old story. If you go to Paris from New York and you work in Paris, you're an international star. If you move to Paris, you're a local. It goes from a thousand dollars a night to seventy-five dollars a night. So Chet kept moving.

He also had a girlfriend the last five or six years named Diane, and she was a very nice person from the San Francisco Bay area. I think she lived in Santa Cruz, and he would stay with her. They would both use drugs, though, and they would fight a lot. It was pretty messy. Anybody that wants to get involved with somebody like Chet – he really was in essence a very lovely, very intelligent, very nice person, but when he had to get heroin he would become very forceful. He had to get the money and he had to get the heroin; I guess it was a matter of life and death, basically.

Chet settled briefly in NY and Jim became his manager and representative.

Being his representative, managing his affairs in New York, wasn't easy. First of all, we never knew if Chet would show up. And then if he showed up, we wouldn't know if he could actually play the trumpet or stand up or be coherent. There's an old adage in the bebop world: no nodding on the bandstand. Chet always nodded on the bandstand. So number one, would he show up? Number two, would he show up on time? Number three, would he be able to play?

I think there was a certain segment of patrons that went to see Chet Baker and would hope to see him fall off the bandstand. They were there to see a trainwreck. They were there to see an execution, more than to come and hear brilliant improvised jazz. Like Sid Vicious, that type of situation, where the people would be fascinated by someone falling apart in front of their eyes.

Working with Chet meant that I had to make sure I had a trumpet for him and that I had a place for him to stay. The last time he stayed in New York, November of 1986, he was at the Tudor Hotel down in East 42nd Street. He was in really bad shape: he had an abscess in his hip because he was shooting up there. The bass player he was playing with at the time – I won't mention any names because the guy's cleaned up his act now – OD'd in the elevator, and they threw Chet out of the hotel. I arranged for my friend Dr Fred Chan, a surgeon, to take care of him. He stayed at Fred's apartment up on 181st Street.

There were other problems. Chet was a brilliant musician; he had a brilliant ear. If he didn't like the musicians that were on the stand he would call me and say, 'Get me a new piano player.' And sometimes he was absolutely justified. The guy that we got him on the last time he played at the Whippoorwill was a guy named Kenny Kirkland; very famous piano player, but a big crack-head. He's dead now. He was laughing throughout the whole set, and he was playing the wrong chord changes.

There are similarities between what Bebop Jim needed to help organise Chet Baker's schedule and running a hi-fi store. Being prepared for the unexpected was one of them.

It's the same thing that I have here. I send my guys out to do installations; I know they're going to fail a lot. It's just reality. I studied Eastern philosophy for twenty-three years. The word is frustration, but knowing that a certain premise will add up to a certain conclusion. If you take a junkie that doesn't give a shit, what are you going to get? I'm not talking not giving a shit about the music, but about his life. They're totally consumed by drugs, and the amount of money it takes.

Now Chet could do a two-week tour in Europe and actually make sixty thousand dollars. In this country he would just basically have rich friends that would lend him money, or fans that would give. There were musicians everywhere that wanted to hang out with Chet and they would buy him drugs. There was no way in the world that I would ever know where to get heroin in New York. I wouldn't be interested in that. But in terms of money – I would always make sure that he had money.

I was his liaison with the club owners in New York. There was one guy that was very interesting, named Duane Tetford. He's dead now. He was one of the most interesting scoundrels in the jazz world. Duane had the knack of being able to talk people who owned restaurants and clubs into thinking that if they became jazz-club impresarios they would make a fortune. He would talk them into hiring Stan Getz for forty thousand dollars a week; Miles Davis for seventy thousand a week. Every place went out of business, and it wasn't his money. The band would be paid. The restaurateur would pay the band out of their own pocket and they would lose money. And eventually they would go out of business and Duane would disappear to the next club. The last club that he was involved with was a place called Condons, not to be confused with Eddie Condon's, which was a Dixieland place in the forties and fifties. A nice man called John Condon, who was a printer and loved jazz, opened a place on 15th Street downtown. Duane bankrupted and ruined this guy, but they had excellent jazz there all the way through.

The last place Chet worked in New York was a place called the Whippoorwill, which was in the basement of a restaurant on 18th Street called Joanna's. The Whippoorwill was the most lavish jazz club I've ever seen. If you went into the men's room they actually had gold handles on the urinals; it was just an amazing place. Duane forgot one little detail though: he didn't have a cabaret licence. He would hire Chet and no one would know Chet was there because he couldn't advertise. But this is where Bruce Weber found Chet, and I arranged for this engagement.

Bruce Weber is a famous fashion photographer. It's no secret that he's gay, and I think he had a big crush on Chet when Chet was young. At the Whippoorwill, an entourage pulled up one night, a bunch of Cadillacs, and Bruce Weber was there with his models. He was so thrilled to see Chet Baker; I guess it's like if my wife met Paul McCartney. He started hanging around the club, and he came up with an idea that he would make a documentary on Chet Baker's life.

Bruce Weber flew him out to LA. He stayed at the

Shangri La Hotel in Santa Monica, which is a very quaint hotel: they have toasters on the tables, I mean silly things. Bruce didn't know how to deal with Chet in any way, shape, form or manner. He gave him too much money: he was giving him two thousand dollars a day. He had my trumpet, by the way. I loaned him a trumpet and it's the one that's in the movie. Chet was basically incoherent. He could hardly talk, and he couldn't play that well. They had to go to the south of France, where Chet was, and they finished the movie there. They had already learned not to give him any more money. Whenever you're dealing with anybody that has habits like that, you have to control the money flow.

So Chet realised that there was a little bit more notoriety. He was making more money playing, and he died before the movie was released. I don't know what that would have done if he was alive. I said, 'Do you think you can see him sitting on David Letterman's couch, or Johnny Carson's couch?' Who knows?

But his life really didn't change much, except he wasn't in the United States much the last year or two. He called me from Paris, called me from Rome, and he was just doing his thing.

For years he couldn't play in Japan because of his drug record; the Japanese are very strict about things like that. You can ask Paul McCartney about that. At any rate, he finally got to Japan in 1986, and it was an overwhelming success. He went back the next year, in June of 1987, and there's a video that's available of his Tokyo tour. He went over with a methadone prescription, he didn't drink, he didn't do anything but maintain himself with methadone for a sixteen-day tour. He looks great and plays great; the videos prove it. That isn't what Chet wanted. He wanted to stay high, and he didn't really care how he looked.

Chet had done a tour of Germany in April of 1988 and Willi Geipel, a friend of mine from Frankfurt who owned the Jazz Keller, showed me some pictures. He said, 'Man, Chet looks like hell. Jim, Chet really doesn't look well.' I thought I would see Chet though; I thought he'd be back in New York probably in the summer. He would come through twice a year, something like that. But after November of 1986, he didn't come back to New York at all, except flying through. He never played here again.

Towards the end, there was another problem. This is what I hear from Gerry Teekens, the owner of Criss Cross Records, who's a big jazz guy out in Holland. There was a fellow that supposedly was the friend of the musicians, but he was really a heroin dealer that lived in Rotterdam. He allowed Chet Baker and Woody Shaw, another very great trumpet player, one of the greatest trumpet players of all time, to live together with him there. It's interesting: Woody Shaw died, almost a year after Chet fell out of the window, of Aids in Newark, New Jersey. If anybody has seen what Chet looked like the last month or two before he died, he didn't look well at all. I'm not just talking the normal dishevelled look of someone without teeth, I'm talking about someone that looked very sick. So who knows? Junkies still shared needles.

There was an article in the *New York Times* back in the sixties, written by a competent medical authority, that said an intravenous dripping of heroin into your bloodstream for the rest of your life would never kill you: wasn't the heroin, it was the life. Although I understand it probably will affect the liver after a while, I think that it's dangerous to be addicted to anything and of course it will most likely extract some sort of physical toll, but not to the extent that most drug addicts die in this country.

Chet had very strong Okie blood. Richard Avedon, the famous photographer, took pictures – and Chet gave me them – of Chet in his underwear. This is 1986. He had the perfect, trim body of a twenty-year-old, and he was fifty-seven years old at the time. When they did the autopsy, when he fell out of the window in Amsterdam, Holland, on May thirteenth 1988, the medical examiner said, 'thirty-five-year-old man,' and he was fifty-eight when he died. So he was really a strong guy, and if he was coherent, no one could touch him in the soulful, beautiful way that he played the trumpet.

First and foremost Chet played jazz. He was not a talker.

First of all, most jazz musicians don't have the skill, or have not developed the skill, of communicating verbally. They're not well read, they're not well written in many cases. Chet was a brilliant guy, but he was focused on drugs; and he was focused on being in control.

The ways to the means was to work. This would mean that he would control the band and sometimes short the band – not pay them as much money as other people would pay them – so he would have more money for his drugs. He would get musicians that would either do it because they loved him, or because he knew he could take control of the situation and not pay them what they were worth.

He was egocentric to the point that you could talk to him about things that he was involved in, like a photo shoot that he had done. He would talk about his physical state, and how he could play the trumpet; you could talk to him at that level. And he could also bring back things from the past about people that he had worked with, like Stan Getz for example. He wasn't a baseball fan; you didn't have anything like that to talk to him about. You could talk to him about where he was and everything, but it was very uncomfortable because he was not living well.

I asked Jim if he'd ever thought of selling him one of his amazing stereos.

Oh no, he had no money to buy a stereo. My wife at the time, he would ask about her, of course. And he would remember my cousin Joanie, things like that. But he was basically in the present at all times. And he was always travelling; he would never be anywhere too long. This guy, he'd had a horrible life. When you think about what he had to do from say 1957 until 1988, he was just living at the edge. He had to get thousands of dollars a week for his habit. He had to keep moving.

He never did anything like steal. He wasn't a second-storey man, he wasn't a murderer, but he had to use his wits to get money for this lifestyle and this habit. And the only thing he could do would be Chet Baker. He was Chet Baker, and he had to play Chet Baker. That's who he was. And remember, this evolved and developed from a nice, sweet kid in 1953 to a guy that was hardened and had done everything to survive. I really think he fell out of the window – he didn't try to kill himself. If he wanted to kill himself, he had better ways of doing it. On the other hand, we knew he wasn't going to die on social security.

Jim was devastated when he heard that Chet had died.

I felt horrible. I loved to hear him play the trumpet: it was just a wonderful thing. Chet Baker was the greatest. I loved him. It was horrible because you didn't expect it to happen that prematurely.

Jim gave support to Chet's family. Then Chet's widow swung into action to start the management of his estate.

He had his wife, he had his daughter, and he had his two sons in Oklahoma. They all came to New York after he died. They were at my apartment and I took them around.

His wife became very much aware of what his catalogue was worth, and she started what is known as the Chet Baker Foundation at this point. I helped her originally. We got some records out; got some tapes and she put the records out. You cannot find Chet Baker on YouTube unless she has something to do with it, and she is making a lot of money now. She controls everything. Paul is one of his sons, and I think he works with her. The other kid, Dean, has problems. He thinks he was abducted by flying saucers. Nice kid, though. Nice people. Hey, it's a total different lifestyle living in Oklahoma; can you imagine what that's like?

He would've returned [to New York]. It was only a matter of time, but it didn't happen. See, he was doing very well in Europe and he didn't have to come back. After the Bruce Weber thing, people were becoming more aware of Chet Baker. He had a big dry spell there until 1988, until he died. [*Laughs*] His dry spell started in like 1957 and it was a thirty-year dry spell.

Chet *had* to work. He would sign away all the rights of every record. There are probably more Chet Baker records out there than there are Beatles records, but he would sell away the rights. The guy would get him in the studio, 'Here's a thousand, here's two thousand dollars, sign this paper, and that's it.'

This is why his wife is having so much trouble getting royalties. But this is what he did, and this is how he made his money. He had to tour, and he had to keep working.

Chet is gone, but Bebop Jim is still running his hi-fi shop in

New York and thinks of the golden days, when jazz was flourishing and evolving.

I have an affinity towards the Caribbean. We have a house down in the Grenadines now. I have to keep working here. I have a couple of ex-wives and I have kids, and that's basically the situation.

What impressed me more than anything about Chet is that he had the total respect of the black jazz musicians, the great musicians. He was not treated as a second-rate 'ofay' [a cant term used by black musicians to describe white musicians trying to be black] trumpet player. I think of him as one of the great trumpet players, one of the great musicians. The guy had his own style, and this is the key to any great jazz artist: can you listen to them and know who it is?

Today, these kids are going to jazz college and they all sound like someone else. Chet really evolved and developed his own style. He started with the Miles Davis language of 1953, but he went from there: the phrasing, the voice, the emotion, the harmonics . . . again, the phrasing. And remember the way he sang: he could scat sing [improvised non-lyric singing] as well as he could play the trumpet. He could play what he could sing and he could sing what he could play. Many times his voice had a very beautiful clarity and purity and emotion to it.

If you need convincing you should listen to Chet Baker singing 'My Funny Valentine'. Unlike some of the many over-embroidered renditions of the song by jazz singers, his interpretation remains for many the defining, pure-toned, master version (see youtube.com/watch?v=jvXywhJpOKs).

There's a record label in Italy: Philology. They put out a record of eight different versions of Chet singing 'My

Funny Valentine', but of course the original one was the one he did with Gerry Mulligan in 1954. Tom Brokaw, who was a big newscaster in the United States for many, many years, came in here in the early eighties and he told me how he had interviewed Carly Simon. He congratulated her on her version of 'My Funny Valentine', and she said, 'No one can do it like Chet.' And that's coming from Carly Simon. Interesting, huh?

The guy was a brilliant musician. Of course we think about him, but all the videos are there, all the CDs, all the records. It's amazing, though. It's hard to believe he died twenty-one years ago. He really lived the life of a jazz musician, but he never stopped improvising or stopped playing well. It didn't matter that he tried to do something else, he always played.

When you look at the lifestyle he had to lead, I don't think he could do it without using drugs. How could you want to just live a crappy life in third-rate hotels all over the world without having any material support? Maybe if you didn't have that barrier between the physical harsh realities and your trumpet playing, maybe you couldn't do it. I don't know.

3

I Was Will Carling's Osteopath

When I had a clinic at the Harbour Club, we had
press literally climbing over the walls to get in and take
photographs and so on.

Will Carling was one of the most talented and controversial
rugby players ever to lead the English rugby union team. He
was appointed captain in 1988, aged just twenty-two, at a time
when the sport was morphing from an enthusiastic league
of amateur teams into a corporate pick 'n' mix of professional outfits, when the importance of money was beginning
to outstrip the simple pleasures of 'a thug's game played by
gentlemen'.

Playing rugby can result in serious impact injuries followed
by long stretches of recuperation or, worse, premature retire-
ment from the game. Long-term effects include depression
and chronic pain. Will Carling's injuries, however, generated far
less press than speculation about his personal life.

Despite being the first and youngest captain to take the
England team to two consecutive Five Nations Grand Slam
victories (1991 and 1992, followed by another in 1995) and
the Rugby World Cup final (1991), it was his public description in 1995 of the England Rugby Football Union Selection
Committee as 'fifty-seven old farts' standing in the way of his
and other players' careers, juggling day jobs with the demands
of amateur rugby and new professional championships, that
propelled him into the limelight.

Nick Potter, a gifted sports osteopath, has worked with

many great sportsmen, including Pete Sampras in his role as osteopath at the Wimbledon Championships. He treated Will Carling for various injuries during his time as England captain, together with the stress that followed the defeat by Australia in the 1991 World Cup final and the endless speculation in the media about his private life.

As a boy, Nick sustained a major injury playing rugby, his childhood passion. The trauma affected him greatly, but also stimulated his desire to understand and treat those who had suffered similarly.

*

I was very lucky to have the privileged background of being privately educated. I went to St Paul's in London, which actually gave me a fantastically meritocratic education. I was very sporty there, and they indulged all my sporting interests. I was in St Paul's Firsts, and Captain of Rugby. I was a big hulk in those days, and if you were in the first fifteen, invariably you were then put in the school boat at number six, pulling on an oar, thumping away; which I actually found incredibly dull, looking at the back of someone's head all day and getting up at six in the morning. I went on to play for Rosslyn Park, and then had a junior cap for schoolboys' rugby, so really it was a passion of mine.

Sadly, some time later, between school and medical school, I had a spinal injury, which is really what changed my career path back into osteopathic medicine. In those days I used to play in the front row, and was unfortunately in a collapsed scrum which occurred in New Zealand. I injured two discs in my back, but also suffered a hairline stress fracture to my lower back, which took some time to rehabilitate from.

It was a terrible blow, because I was looking very seriously at going on playing rugby, and in fact was due to go on to play for London Wasps [a professional rugby union team based in High Wycombe] to take my career forward. The injury stopped that happening.

I'd been doing sciences all the way through; that was my fascination. It's always been in my blood: in our family we're all either lawyers or doctors. My involvement in the medical pathway probably meant I had less time. I had to – as so many of us did in those days, pre-professionalism – make a decision about what I actually wanted to do: follow a career or stay in sport.

I'm rather pleased I've followed the way I have. Sometimes I look back and think maybe I'd have liked to stay in hospital medicine, but actually a lot of my colleagues who I trained with and have gone on to become consultants, are very unhappy in the NHS system, and are very, very demoralised by medicine. That's why so many of them are going abroad now.

The experience I had, and the shock that I realised with other patients when I saw them, was that too many of the diagnostic procedures in sports injuries were being left to pretty under-qualified physiotherapists. Not that they were under-qualified as physiotherapists, but they weren't qualified to be making proper neurological assessments, particularly in spinal injuries.

Jonny Wilkinson is a very good example. For months he was going on, supposedly being treated for a shoulder injury, but in fact he had a nerve root irritation in his neck that was causing compression to a nerve. Of course, it really set him back. He continued to do damage to his neck every time, and ended up having to have quite significant surgery to rectify what was really a bad neck, not a bad shoulder. But for too long physios were making those medical determinations on what the treatment should be and who he should see.

Now, with professionalism growing, we're seeing team doctors taking over from physios. It is only in the last two years, with the resurgence of the Olympics, that sports medicine has actually become a speciality. There is only, so far [as of 2009], one consultant post in Britain set up purely and simply to deliver sports medicine, which is a very specialist area. It's not just orthopaedics and musculoskeletal injury. It's all about performance and diet, and generally how you train athletes in a globally expanding world of sport.

One of the major keys to medicine generally – and what I like about osteopathic medicine particularly – is it really is about treating the patient; not the imaging or the symptoms that come in. You do have to have a kind of intuitiveness, and read people. Most importantly, what brings people through my door, whether it's fractures or dislocations or injury or just long-term problems, is really pain, and pain is a fascinating subject.

We still know very little about it in real terms. New forms of MRI scanning are allowing us to look at what pain does to people and which parts of the brain light up, and it's rather surprised us that it's not what we thought. It very quickly, with time, goes from a simple sort of evolutionary response to pull away from the stimulus for the pain, right through to actually becoming very intensely depressed, institutionalised by their pain. They become sociophobic and retract from having to do things that are obviously painful. It very quickly affects their libido, their general approach to work, their love life, etc.

So what starts as a physical ailment becomes a long-term psychological one?

It becomes a global problem, absolutely.

I think really it was just proving it. Inevitably there were patients who were falling through the net of the sub-specialisation, which is endemic in medicine now; where if their symptoms didn't slot into the particular speciality that they were presenting to, for example, a neurologist or a surgeon, the surgeon would basically declare he couldn't do anything and then send them on. Really, they'd end up just floating around in the ether. So a lot of people tend to find a path to your door through recommendation. Most of my patients come to me through word of mouth because 'This guy fixed me and I had a similar problem and the other doctors failed me.'

It's not Einsteinian: osteopathic medicine is much more about treating function rather than anatomy and that sort of thing. So you may call a neurologist a software specialist and an orthopaedic surgeon a hardware specialist. To be honest with you, we're the technicians; we kind of match the two together. Unless there's a gross anatomical deformity and that sort of thing, then medicine very often falls short of being able to treat people; and that's really where osteopathic medicine comes in.

But a new area of medicine can bring the risk that your peers may choose not to recognise your work.

In America, funnily enough, we osteopaths have a much greater standing, and actually there are whole osteopathic hospitals. A lot of the old principles have been lost in our bid to become recognised, and regulated; sadly more and more. It's limiting the art of the medicine rather than simply the science, and this perennial problem of litigation really changes the way people practise their art. They're constantly wanting to back themselves up with imaging and so on. And imaging and tests are very often very unreliable. They're very gross in their ability to pick up fine changes in people since, by definition, an image is static.

Indeed, in the old days you could actually be struck off as a doctor for referring to the likes of an osteopath. I think now they've understood that we have a proper medical training, there's a much greater level of understanding.

Of course, they couldn't ignore the fact that the patients that did still choose to come and see an osteopath seemed to be getting better. They could only put that down to placebo for so long. Now we are doing osteopathic contracts with the NHS, which is very exciting.

But there's still a long way to go. I don't think that osteopathy holds all the answers, and I still continue to train in lots of other approaches and travel the world looking at other ways of approaching techniques and so on. It's about having a toolbox from which you can pick the tool that you need to treat the individual problem. You've got to have an amazing grounding in generalism, and then if you want to sub-specialise, that's fine, but you've still got to be able to assess people properly.

Nick's own rugby injury, knowledge, confidence and unique abilities in this area brought him to the attention of professional sportsmen bearing injuries, including Will Carling.

Because I had developed a busy practice quite quickly in my career, I was unable to travel with sportsmen as I used to, which was mostly in golf, tennis, Formula 1 and a lot of rugby players and teams. So then I began to only really consult to them when they had specific problems that weren't being dealt with at the sharp end. Will ended up on my doorstep through a number of recommendations. It was really word of mouth, but also through, I suppose, having a degree of reputation amongst the sports world.

I saw him for a very specific injury. Most injuries received by centres and tacklers are very different from those in the scrum. The scrum are usually built like brick . . . you know like houses, and therefore can take a lot of hits and are designed to be very strong. Unfortunately, the high impact that is received at speed is much greater in centres and people who are tackling; and very often asymmetrical: they very often always tackle with one shoulder. Someone like Mickey Skinner sadly is now having terrific problems with his right side because he always tackled with the same shoulder.

A lot of them are very obsessive about knocking a guy back rather than actually just tackling him, and that is a big problem. The combined forces have actually been calculated to be up in the region of several tonnes when they get hit. And they're playing up to forty-two times a year, compared, for example, with the All Blacks, who actually only play about twenty-eight times a year. So these guys are having to meet the demands of this impact, and some players would have blood in their urine after a match. It means they're getting high levels of soft-tissue injury, from which they're having to recover very quickly within a week.

Understanding what the individual positions required was very different, because the backs were predominantly tackling. Wing forwards again were tackling, but were also having to provide enormous amounts of power, so they had a different type of fitness, a different type of strength. If you went into the scrumming positions, hookers and front row forwards have enormous amounts of load put through their necks and their spines generally. A lot of the load is asymmetrical, so you have to know which side they're playing and so on.

Also, simple things like hydration: we now know much more about the processes. If people get increasingly dehydrated during a game they're much more likely to injure, which won't be evident for a number of years.

Managing Will Carling's physio on a day-to-day level when he was captain of England was not Nick's responsibility, but could he help with things like special injuries?

Because I couldn't be there with the daily things, I tended to see him for a course of treatment at my practice, and then periodically when we built a trust and he wanted to come back and see me about other things. Predominantly, the day-to-day stuff was done by the team physios and doctors.

The early nineties were an interesting time for rugby. It was pupating from a vigorous, noble, principally amateur sport into a money-making, star-manufacturing, professional one. Will Carling cut a dashing pathway through this transitional period with all the passion of a young fly-half.

He was at a very interesting cusp for British rugby – well, for all international rugby. The cross into professionalism had just occurred very recently. The pressures were building with the other forms of championships that were beginning to develop: the Super 12s of this world and so on. The crossover was all very difficult. Most of these guys were still holding down jobs and were being allowed time away, but equally had to make a living. The level of training and the kind of specialist training was still very poor. People think that first-class rugby or football employs the best people, but sadly it's still very often the case that it's jobs for the boys and friends of friends and this sort of thing. That is all changing now, but that certainly wasn't the case then; getting access to good high-level treatment was very tricky.

The pressures of that were enormous. There was also enormous pressure to take performance-enhancing drugs, which I certainly know most of these guys were resisting, but I would suspect not so much now. As the teams got bigger and the pressures got harder and the bid to recover got worse, that is certainly huge pressure. If you're then captain of a team, you're having to look at your own leadership skills, your own self-doubt, your own self-confidence. A lot of rugby players are ex-public school. I think they have a very high level of confidence, but very often grounded on very little.

When they begin to see the leadership not working, they become very inward. They can't share their normal worries with the rest of the team because that shows up their doubts. What Clive Woodward did so well in his team was that he created enormous amounts of trust between each other, and discretion; and secrecy to a certain extent. If people in the team were writing articles all the time, you didn't know who you could trust, and that creates a huge doubt on your own performance.

We know much more about sports psychology. Will is, or certainly was, incredibly durable on that side of things. He was very able to bury his stress, and was able to show it. I'm sure internally he was wrangling enormously. He also had lots of stuff going on in his personal life which made things very difficult, lots of comment about his marriage and so on. Certainly that takes its toll, and it is manifested musculoskeletally. You will see people; they're tenser when they come in, they're less able to relax generally, so you end up helping to treat not just their physical problems, but their performance generally at a physical and psychological level. Inevitably, from the confidentiality side of things, people build up a trust with you, and you do discuss things with them. So you can, if you're not careful, become a shrink as much as anything else, which you have to be careful not to overindulge in.

I think the fact that I was independent from the team did help because Carling didn't have to worry that any of it would go back to the internal management. When people are stressed we know that the pain levels increase and that they're more likely to injure. With hindsight, I think that decisions made on the pitch certainly don't help, particularly if the results don't work out: it makes you more introspective. Certainly, I think he was more agitated during that period. Again, you have to manage that, help him manage it and manage his injuries within.

To say whether it helped his confidence, yes, I think it was a secondary effect. It was an ability to dump, an ability to offload, and also perhaps to give him insight into why he's not getting better. The length of his recovery was based much more on the fact that actually he wasn't in a healing environment, and wasn't putting himself under the best possible environment to get better, rather than because he was failing as an individual, failing in his ability. His body wasn't failing him. These guys have very fragile confidence, and when they see the self-doubt creep in, it's very difficult to recover from.

I think it's more the obsessive external interest from the media. When I had a clinic at the Harbour Club, we had press literally climbing over the walls to get in and take photographs and so on. That is intensely frustrating and it's there with you twenty-four hours a day: they're following you. Not to mention the fact that it has an effect on marriages and relationships and all those things. If your home base is also affected, then I think your ability to go out and do your daily work, in any job, particularly if it's operating at a high performance level like that, is fundamentally affected. It does make you agitated and less able to make leadership decisions.

Being captain is like being a CEO athlete or a corporate athlete, really, in the sense they are managing. They're not just the captain; they're really setting up a management structure in what is now a growing industry, a corporate environment. Very often it's fifteen individuals trying to get on, managing their own careers, rather than actually a team. That's something Will and a number of people have learned since, that if you're really going to create an unstoppable force in the form of an England team, you actually have to create the team-ness, the bonding-ness – which again is more psychological and based on trust than it is on anything to do with their physical performance.

I thought he was a very mentally strong and able chap; I was pleasantly surprised. He was very well equipped for handling what was a very difficult period in the England team: the number of transitions that were occurring, handling a very dominant southern hemisphere force, trying to change the thinking.

Will Carling's unfortunate reference to the Rugby Football Union Committee as 'fifty-seven old farts' got him sacked, but an apology and intense public pressure saw him reinstated.

I think the reference to the fifty-seven farts probably wasn't unfair, and some would argue still applies. Until the consciousness in British rugby changes to be more like the southern hemisphere, we're always going to be beaten by them. It's because it's an absolutism; it's a godlike belief in themselves, but also in the team as a unit. More importantly it's about not allowing individualism: it's a group of fifteen men rather than these individuals. We have it in football. They're becoming personalities, which in New Zealand rugby isn't allowed to happen.

How would Carling's situation compare with that of Pete Sampras, who as a tournament tennis player had to stand alone against a competitor? There is no one else on your team when you are on the tennis court, facing match point from one opposing force on the other side of the net.

I think Pete would admit – and so would a number of people that know him – he's a very cool, icy customer. These guys, rather than dwelling on the last shot which went wrong, will very easily simply make the next one right.

The guys who think too much about the last shot, and what they did wrong, will simply go on to make more mistakes. Most of sport is a neuroprogram. They're so able to make the same shot fifty times, without thinking about it, that the out-of-the-bag shot is the one that you consciously change.

In some ways, in a team sport it's easier because you have the support of your colleagues to say, 'Don't worry, old chap, it's just a bad day.' But with isolated sports like tennis, and golf particularly – of all of them golf stands out – it is much more difficult to cope without endurance, pace and hardship. And it is difficult if you haven't got that innate programming, and also the ability to simply take criticism and take it from yourself, and why he may be not just playing well but why you're playing badly – the psychology is very intense. If there's a commonality between the big players, it is this single-mindedness, this total belief in themselves, and a lack of introspection in some ways; the ability to simply make the next shot great and not think about the last one.

For those suffering with old rugby injuries that have left them with titanium rods sticking through their kneecaps, managing the ongoing ageing process and the pain that gathers is getting slightly easier – but only slightly.

It's a big question, but to summarise it I would say that certainly in rugby, in most sports, yes, the science is coming in. This is where the sports medicine, sports science, is making a big difference: our greater understanding of what makes our bodies and muscles work, the importance of diet and hydration. But more importantly, if old problems are coming back to haunt them, they're not better.

This is the biggest problem in sport. The pressure to get back into playing is so great, particularly with the demands of money and management – that and their percentage – that the biggest battle is very often actually remembering that the player is your patient, not the management structure, and that your relationship is entirely with them. You must advise them on what is going to make them better in the long term as much as in the short term. And being strong enough – and a lot of this just comes from experience, and having some balls, really – to say, 'Look, instead of putting a plaster on this for three weeks, you actually need six months off. You need complete R & R, and you need a recovery strategy, but also rehabilitation and then a strengthening strategy. For the sake of six months now, you will benefit from having the next five to ten years symptom- and injury-free.'

That's why we're seeing even golfers becoming elite athletes. Even cricketers now are highly conditioned athletes. They just don't produce the number of injuries for the level and intensity at which they play. So if anyone's carrying an injury, they're not being treated and managed properly. It's as simple as that.

I was concerned. Surely there is a problem here. How could Nick be so passionate about sports injuries whilst endorsing the very team game that promulgates them?

Interestingly, a number of research studies have shown that in rugby the number of spinal injuries actually is incredibly low for the number of impacts and things like that, which is good. It shows that increasingly, even at social levels of rugby, levels of fitness, levels of training, levels of conditioning and discipline are getting much greater, and therefore those injuries are getting less.

Ironically, for all of the injuries I've had – and my back wasn't the only one, there were several other broken bones and so on – I wouldn't change it for the world. Socially I had a fantastic time. The camaraderie I don't think you ever get over. And even when you're retired it remains with you. You have your reunions, they stay mates for ever.

I think also, particularly with men, less so with women possibly, you need that laddishness. You need to go away, be male, pump off some testosterone, talk rubbish to your mates, do the drinking afterwards. It's a catharsis as much as it is actually just about winning, and I think that's important. We are losing that now. It's about enjoyment much more.

It seems madness, and again it is psychology in the sense that you've got to be able to throw yourself at a brick wall and not worry about it. Some will just say that it's inanely stupid, which I probably agree with, but it's also hugely enjoyable. As I say, you can do lots to minimise the potential for injury, and increasingly now there are less spinal injuries and much more on peripheral joints like knees.

Unfortunately, we're seeing many more people in sport generally. You can argue that in our bid to try and become cardiovascularly more healthy, we're also increasing the number of orthopaedic injuries and disability, so there is an issue there.

Performance enhancers are becoming a big problem in sport. Most of the great baseball achievements in the nineties by Sammy Sosa and Barry Bonds have now been discredited after their alleged use of steroids. What is to be done?

It's very simple. My answer is, it absolutely should be banned and not recognised or allowed, because the evidence shows that kids as young as nine are now using it, and this is why we shouldn't be using it. The side effects of these drugs are in general terms appalling and are underplayed: everything from osteoporosis to psychosis. One of the reasons it might be attractive to rugby players is that certain steroids not only increase levels of aggression and muscle mass, but also aid recovery.

Anabolic steroids; they even advocate certain painkillers. Drugs like cocaine and amphetamine. Cycling is renowned for still being rife with it. I truly believe that until the governing bodies really have an interest in wiping it out, we'll always see it happening. And until we can enforce blood testing, most of our urine testing's a waste of time. We can't enforce blood tests because of human-rights issues. Unfortunately, even in blood testing, quite high levels, certainly of growth hormone, are almost undetectable.

Nick has a simple message for victims of casual violence – or rugby, as it's known in the medical profession.

Listen to the patient first. See where the pain's coming from and how long it's been there. But also really, see what it's stopping them doing. Understand it, be empathic to it. And then educate them about it.

I think the most important thing is it's a therapeutic relationship. Rather than simply telling them what they should be doing, make this a dual relationship about understanding and education – what they can be doing when you're not actually treating them. How they can improve their lifestyles even if it's just to come off things until they make a way forward. Teach them pacing, not doing too much – they can do certain things, but don't do too much of it. Having realistic goals, and also helping them understand that actually there is an answer, rather than becoming very black about the possibility that there is no way forward.

4

I Was Billie Holiday's Stand-in at the Apollo in Harlem

Annie? I want to get some jewellery for my daddy.

The singer Billie Holiday – Lady Day, as she was named by her regular saxophonist and cohort Lester Young – introduced an entirely new level of emotional 'inscape' to popular singing, as well as bringing a distinctive approach to the technical side of vocalising for the ever-widening genre of mid-twentieth-century jazz and popular music. Billie's personal life was traumatic and savage. A heroin addict since the forties, she also endured the horror of Catholic reform school. Her first break as a singer came when she sang with Benny Goodman in 1933, going solo in 1936. Leaving the Brunswick label for Columbia she sang 'Strange Fruit', the song that would define her and her career. Many did not appreciate the significance of the lyrics, based on a poem by a schoolteacher from the Bronx about a lynching: 'Southern trees bear a strange fruit, Blood on the leaves and blood at the root'.

Some of Billie Holiday's best-known songs include 'God Bless the Child', 'Don't Explain' and 'Lady Sings the Blues'. She frequently made appearances at Harlem's Apollo Theatre in the forties and fifties with various big bands, including those of Duke Ellington and Count Basie.

Annie Ross was a singer, too. She was born on 25 July 1930.

*

I was born while my parents were touring their Scottish vaudevillian routine round London, in Mitcham, Surrey, after a matinee. They [my parents] performed at the Empire Theatre, Edgware Road. The act was comedy and music; Father played accordion, my mother sang. They were a hit, but because of financial circumstances my parents had to work all the time and were performing right up to within hours of when I was born in the Mitcham house in Surrey, called Loch Lomond. After that we went straight back to Glasgow, where my mother and father lived and had three boys, then we went to America, to vacation with my aunt Ella Logan, and she, to her credit, bought me my first record, which was Ella Fitzgerald, 'A Tisk and a Task'. I didn't know what she was singing, I didn't know it was jazz, I just knew that I wanted to sing like that.

At four and a half years old, Annie felt a natural affinity with the singers she was hearing at the time. But it would be ten years before she heard Billie Holiday singing for the first time.

I first heard Billie when I was about fourteen. My aunt introduced me to Mildred Bailey [American jazz singer of the thirties]. Then my uncle bought a record collection which included Billie Holiday singing 'Strange Fruit'. Accompanied by Billy Eckstein, it was an eye and ear opener. I felt the greatest thing to do when you want to do something like singing is to listen. So I listened to everything I could get. By that time my aunt Ella was a singer. She knew Duke Ellington, who came over to the house, and I sang for him, Roy Eldridge and Erroll Garner.

Duke Ellington was genuinely delighted with Annie's singing.

He was amazed not only at the voice but the fact that I knew an obscure Duke Ellington song. He couldn't believe I was doing what I was doing.

Annie used her singing technique to flatter the Duke.

Of course, *I* knew what I was doing.

But it would be a while before Annie would get her first break. As she matured into a singer of unique quality herself, she was drawn increasingly to the rare beauty of Billie's talent. 'Strange Fruit' had had a profound impact on her.

Especially when I was younger. My aunt and I were travelling in North Carolina and we got out of the plane so it could refuel, and there was a chain gang working in fields near the airport and my aunt said, 'Never forget that – that's evil,' so when I heard 'Strange Fruit' it touched me.

My first break was in London in a private club, the Orchid Room off Bond Street, but it was so snobbish it was horrible; they wouldn't allow me to sit in the room when I wasn't singing. However, I was singing a lot of Rodgers and Hart, Cole Porter and after a while they got me a little light – a spotlight – and then I built up a coterie of people who wanted to hear me. At that time there was such controversy about allowing Lena Horne to come into the club with her husband Lennie Heyton, because they didn't allow black people in the club and Lena Horne was black. This was in London at the Orchid Room!

Second-class citizenry was alive and well in the Orchid Room, as well as in the chain gangs of North Carolina. Annie decided it was time to get her own representation. Back in the US, she signed up with Mob agent to the stars, Joe Glaser.

I had just signed with a rough, tough agent called Joe Glaser. I went to see him; it was the most extraordinary meeting. I went with a friend and walked into this room, and there was this little man behind the desk and nobody had come in to say, 'Mr Glaser, this is Annie Ross,' and all of a sudden he looked up and shouted 'Dave!' and I nearly died. 'Get that spot off the wall!' I thought, 'Oh no, how am I going to cope with this?'

'They told me you sing and they told me you're pretty good. Well, we'll see what we can do for you. Sign here!'

So I signed. I don't even know what it was I signed, and that was the end of that and the end of my audience with him. So my girlfriend and I walked out all excited and we proceeded to celebrate being taken on by a high-powered agent. Joe Glaser used to handle Louis Armstrong, Duke Ellington and Billie Holiday. He was an ex-bootlegger from Chicago who raised poodles.

When I got back to Chicago about eight thirty in the morning, the phone rang.

'Annie Ross? This is Joe Glaser . . . Have you got a gown, music?'

I said, 'Yes.'

'Have you got a piano player?'

'I can get one.'

'OK. I want you to take your gown, your music, your piano player and be at the Apollo Theatre in Harlem for the first show.'

I think it started at about 11.30 p.m. 'Great, thank you,' and I went to hang up the phone. 'What am I doing?'

Joe said, 'You're replacing someone.'

'Who?'

'Billie Holiday!' and he hung up the phone.

Well, I was so stunned. It was like being hit over the head with a baseball bat. I did what he said. I went up to the Apollo and the early show was for all the hard nuts. They were like, 'What can you do?' And I was substituting for Billie Holiday!

It was exciting and frightening and all that . . . I was

sitting in my dressing room shaking, and Duke Ellington came in and said, 'Oh, baby, what's the matter?'

I said, 'What's the matter? I'm dying!'

'Have you ever met Lady [Day]?'

'No, and I don't think I want to. If she said anything to me I'd melt.'

'Nonsense!'

He took me to her dressing room. She was packing up stuff. She said, 'Have you got a gown, music and a piano player?' I nodded. Billie said, 'OK. You'll be fine anyway.' We go down to the stage level and Duke got on the mike and said, 'Ladies and gentlemen, Billie Holiday will not be performing the first show.'

There was pandemonium in the audience, as Annie recalls.

A lot of people got out, a lot of people stayed and these were heavy-duty bands.

Duke Ellington continued, 'However, we have a young lady performing . . .'

And the thing that saved my bacon was we were doing things like 'Twisted Jackie', 'Farmers Market', and they [the crowd] loved me. I came off in a stupor into the arms of Billie Holiday, who was standing in the wings because she wanted to check out what was happening. I started to cry, and she started to cry. Ellington said to them, 'You two beautiful ladies have got to go on. Take your bow.' We did, but no one had a camera. That would have been a fantastic picture but that was how it occurred. Duke Ellington and Billie Holiday paid me the compliment of standing there and listening.

It wasn't clear why Billie couldn't do the first show, but for Annie it was an astonishing experience.

You know Lady was a great friend, Diana Washington, Sarah Vaughan . . . the reason we were close was I had such respect. So they saw I wasn't coming on like a square 'ofay' singer.

Annie and Billie became good friends after Annie stood in for her at the Apollo. By this point Billie had become addicted to heroin and the signs were often clear to see.

I saw her in Europe and in New York. She rang me up one day and said, 'Annie, it's my birthday. Will you come up?' Well, to be invited by an idol! So of course I went. She had a small apartment; there were very few people. I remember there was a writer called Leonard Feather, English. He said, 'Annie, don't let this happen to you!'

At the party Billie did not look well.

She was thin as a rake. Feather said she shouldn't go out, she's pretty sick. They put her on a stool. Well, she sang her head off. And then she went into hospital. We called the hospital and we were told she was banned from seeing anybody in case they brought her drugs. I believe New York health authorities and the police killed her. They took away her livelihood because she had convictions.

In spite of her fame and no doubt because of her addiction, Billie had no money. But she liked Annie's music.

She loved Lambert, Hendricks and Ross [Annie Ross's dazzling and successful jazz vocal group]. I was asked if I'd heard any good tunes.

It was Lambert, Hendricks and Ross who put words to 'scat', or improvised vocalising.*

* Think Manhattan Transfer for the forties/fifties and you'll be close. Joni

[76]

'Twisted', a popular song of the fifties, is astonishing, as it sounds so inventive and fresh for its time, with Lambert, Hendricks and Ross singing what would be saxophone and trumpet solos with choruses sung as three-part vocal jazz harmony. Billie loved Annie's band and her scat lyrical ideas.

We sang in clubs together. She could do scat but only when she was fooling.

She was very good with technical phrasing and learned a lot of that from Lester Young. She loved it; she thought it [Annie's band] was great. The music still holds up but when I happen to be somewhere they are playing it, I think it sounds great.

She voiced the blues. She loved cartoons. She could be angry, nasty to people, and I witnessed some scenes, but she was never nasty to me.

Billie was unique and I can only admire and love her.

Annie was able to see the effects touring had on Billie.

She was affronted at some concerts [especially after singing in front of white audiences that hurled abuse at her] and

---

Mitchell covered one of Lambert, Hendricks and Ross's songs, 'Twisted', for her *Court and Spark* album.

Here, on YouTube, is an extract of Lambert, Hendricks and Ross from Hugh Hefner's Network Playboy TV in 1959, with the trio backed by Count Basie's rhythm section: youtube.com/watch?v=e8uMdb-WHwc-&feature=related.

Here's another offering from YouTube explaining Annie's vocal style: youtube.com/watch?v=anrXYEAkg8U&feature=related.

And this is John Hendricks from that trio performing with the Manhattan Transfer in the nineties: youtube.com/watch?v=jkRXl52gHRQ &feature=related.

One of the great exponents of the craft of scat singing was Scatman Crothers. Frequently performing for Al Capone as a young man, Crothers would go on to be one of Jack Nicholson's regular band of actors, appearing in *The King of Marvin Gardens*, Stanley Kubrick's *The Shining* and *One Flew Over The Cuckoo's Nest*, as well as many other films.

it's called rejection, but much of it was the behaviour of some white people and certain practices that were rife in those days. But she was also philosophical, though I'm sure if she'd had a gun she'd have used it. She had insults from the audience.

Was Billie's standing in the black community compromised by working with white musicians?

Maybe so, but not nearly as much as the fact that she was black and in that region.

Away from America, Billie could happily make trouble for herself, as Annie recalls.

She came to Paris. She was wearing a blue mink and a skiing outfit. The hotel was at the Arc de Triomphe off the boulevard and she said, 'Annie, I want to get some jewellery for my daddy.'

I said, 'OK. Do you want to walk down the Champs Elysées?'

'Yes.'

So she put on her mink and we started on the Champs Elysées. We stopped at almost every bar and she was drinking I think brandy with a Pernod float. I drank the same as I wanted to be like my idol.

Well, by the time we got three-quarters down the Champs, I felt really out of it, and she wasn't feeling any pain. We went into a jewellery shop and the man recognised her and brought out these velvet trays of gold charms, and she said to him, 'I need some for my daddy.' I don't know if he knew what daddy meant in this context but he brought out more and more trays, and she said, 'Oh, I don't see anything . . . no, no thank you,' and we walked out.

About two blocks away she said, 'He-he-he-he, look!' She had shoplifted a whole handful of these gold charms and things, and for her it wasn't being a thief, it was a joke. She outsmarted him.

And when Billie turned up as a guest on a radio station in the US she had a special request. Annie discovered this only recently.

I sing once a week in a club in NY. A guy came in one night and said, 'I had a DJ show in Philly and she [Billie Holiday] was on as a guest and all she kept saying was, "Play Annie Ross, play Annie Ross."' Well, can you imagine, can you imagine?

She realised I hadn't had an easy time of it – nothing as bad as her, but you know I think when you really pay respect to someone and it's really and truly meant, it's not put on, they realise full emotion, especially Billie Holiday.

There are singers who don't pay much attention to the words. I always think it does a disservice to a lyric writer if people don't get the words right, even a 'the' or an 'an'.

I've always imagined a songwriter calling up at four in the morning saying, 'I've got it!'

I had a discussion last night with a woman about song-writers and she didn't really get my point. I said, 'I can't bear sloppy songwriting, rhyming words that don't really rhyme.' That's what kills me. I've heard songs – they're good songs, but if you sang them the way they're written it would be awful because there wouldn't be anything that would rhyme properly.

When Annie heard Billie had died she was distressed and angry with the 'authorities'.

We were on tour with Lester Young. We were somewhere

like Boston. I couldn't get to her and, oh my, that was a sad day.

No one was allowed into the hospital to see her in case they were smuggling in drugs. I tried to get into the hospital to see her and they wouldn't let us in. Anybody, not just me . . . so political.

To withdraw from heroin in those conditions, in those days . . . They didn't have rehab, so she must have been in agony because they took that [heroin] away. That's what killed her.

Her closest friend was Bobby Tucker, her pianist, but when they busted her he went with her to jail and went to the trial. He so admired what she did, but nobody had the power to do anything. People in authority didn't understand musicians.

I sang my way through the grief.

My approach didn't change. As you can imagine, I was terribly sad and bereft but I just sang more to try to rid myself of the empty feelings you get when somebody dies.

I feel privileged to have known her, to have been with her, to have laughed with and cried with her.

And to have deputised for her at the Apollo.

Yes . . . Yeah . . . That's a rare experience . . . Like being knighted by the gods, it is . . .

I believed it was important to have great humility. I knew what those singers went through. Awards are nice, but it's what your peers think of you. It's the joy; you get so much joy from music. I have millions of unknown songs from the thirties and forties and I want to sing them all. Our musicians call our Tuesday-night gig 'the teaching school' because I teach them new songs. They are not really new songs but for them they are.

As she said earlier, Annie still sings every week in a New York jazz club.

It's half an hour from my house. I see my band as my children. It's like a little family.

I asked her to give me a burst of song.

I'm travellin' light, because my man's gone, so from now on, I'm travellin' light . . . That's enough.

Annie has a beautiful singing voice for a woman in her eighties, enriched with years of experience, wonder and heartache. It is jazzy, tonally astounding and contemporary. A lot like Billie Holiday, in fact.

5

I Was Ernest Hemingway's
La Secretaría

Writing at its best is a lonely life . . . for he does his work alone; he must face eternity, or the lack of it every day. It is because we have had such great writers in the past that a writer is driven far out past where he can go, out to where no one can help him . . .

Hemingway's radio acceptance speech for the Nobel Prize for Literature, 1954

Ernest Hemingway was one of the most successful American novelists of the twentieth century. In 1954 he was awarded the Nobel Prize for Literature. His life was a self-driven, tortuous one, an endless wrestling match with his own perceived greatness and other writers who might threaten that supremacy. He became one of the greatest contributors to English literature. Along the way he became soaked in alcohol and machismo.

Hemingway's literary journey began as a journalist on the *Kansas City Star* and took him to Europe as a war correspondent to report from Spain during the Spanish Civil War and from Second World War France in 1944. His famously pared-down reporting style probably owed more to practicality than anything else. Getting news out from the front meant shouting copy down a dodgy field phone – there would have been little time for verbosity.

Valerie Danby-Smith, as she then was, was Hemingway's last secretary before he committed suicide in 1961. She was born in Dublin in 1940. When her father left home suddenly in 1943, her mother, burdened with debt and physically and emotionally destroyed, was incapable of caring for her children.

*

When I was three my parents split up. My brother and I were sent off to a convent school; he to the boys' division and I to the girls' school, so I stayed until seventeen and sat for Leaving Certificate. The convent was entirely nuns – being a girls' school, it was entirely run by women. It was like a medieval village. It had a weaving department, a farm, slaughterhouse – everything was done by women; the only man who set foot there officially was the priest, so we treated him with awe.

This was the Irish Free State; free so long as you were a devout Catholic, of course.

Ireland, after it got its freedom from Britain, really embraced the Catholic faith and all its precepts were incorporated in the government. Part of that was the censorship of books. In school we read Dickens, Shakespeare, just a few classics. There was no veering into modern literature, so it was only by chance that I learned books were banned. One of them was Hemingway's *Fiesta: The Sun Also Rises*. That was one of the things that propelled me to go to Spain, reading about this foreign country in fairly modern times. Ireland was still quite antiquated I think and was still in the Victorian era. The school was regimented and dedicated to learning. I'm happy I had such an education. At the hotel [the Summerhill Hotel, a radical, liberal environment where Valerie spent her summer holidays] we were encouraged to have conversations, not read books. I was horrified at the prospect of leaving school at fourteen as I wanted to carry on with education. When you're very contained it increases your imagination, you're prodded to think on your own. I can remember reading poetry that was not on the curriculum, terrified the nuns would discover you were reading whatever it was – it could have been Robert Burns when it should have been Padraig Pearse or Padraic Colum, one of those Irish poets. I think it encouraged, it fostered adventure because we were always trying to get around the rules without breaking them.

Valerie's first encounters with newspapers came from a most unlikely source, and for her became a puzzle to solve.

Instead of using toilet paper, newspapers were cut up, which wasn't unusual in those days. Of course we never saw a newspaper actually in the school as they were forbidden as irrelevant material, and yet in the toilets one only got portions. There was never a full story, so again that made you imagine how things turned out, just little bits and pieces. We were monitored quite closely and you couldn't spend much time in the toilets so I always picked a different stall so I could go back again and get a different sheet of newspaper. I never thought of a newspaper as being one entire thing. I was small when this happened and all I knew was when I went to the toilet you found little pieces of stories sitting in the box.

Valerie's convent was a self-contained environment complete with fitted confessionals, sweeping brides of Christ into a permanent unrequited honeymoon, cocooned in a kind of Catholic 'Center Parcs for sinners', stripped of men . . . apart from the visiting priest.

He came every morning to say Mass and benediction in the evening, and on Sundays and holy days he was there longer. We never really had a close relationship; it was always that awesome thing where you were at a distance. Every Friday we went to confession. Scary experience. We took it seriously, considered our sins and kept half an eye open to see if friends' penance was longer than yours. The number of prayers depended on the seriousness of the sin. You didn't want to let the nun who was guarding you know, so you had to try to say your penance as fast as possible if it was a long one, and then you didn't want to appear you had no sins at all so you'd try to make it a uniform time so as not to allow people to evaluate the state of your soul. Those are the funny things.

There were other men in Valerie's life at this time apart from the visiting monsignor, including her uncle Patrick who was . . . a priest.

That Hemingway and I got on so well was because I'd spent two summers with my uncle priest. He was a very authoritarian figure who was very colourful, loquacious, brilliant, but he scared me very much. And he looked like and had the same shape voice as Orson Welles. With my uncle Patrick I was so scared of making mistakes with him, and he tended to be very sharp if you did. He looked down on the Irish – it was my first foray outside of Ireland in 1956 and he'd invited me to join him in London and go on this pilgrimage to Portugal. But I found all the time I was making faux pas with Uncle Patrick.

Hemingway was also like this but he was a much kindlier person. When I met Hemingway everything I seemed to do was the right thing. So I wasn't intimidated by him. His commanding presence reminded me of Welles too. I greatly admired Orson Welles but it didn't quite work out the same way with my uncle Patrick.

Away from the firm hands of the nuns and her uncle Patrick, Valerie spent her school holidays at the Summerhill Hotel in County Wicklow, where all kinds of colourful characters came and went, from writers, actors, artists, drunkards and charlatans, all the way down to journalists.

A frequent guest was Terry Cronin from New York, wife of Seán Cronin, the IRA's chief of staff. But she was also the founder and editor of *Creation*, the first glossy magazine in Dublin.

Through Terry Cronin, Valerie met other journalists, including Gary McGelligut, then a senior writer on the *Irish Times*, but to get her foot in the door she needed an angle.

I said to McGelligut, 'If I can't get a job here I'll just have to go abroad.' A good friend who'd gone to Spain wrote to me saying, 'You've got to come, we'll have lots of fun.' So I said to McGelligut, 'I'll go to Spain,' and he said, 'Well, that would be the wise thing to do. Go to Spain and send back stories. If I can use them I'll publish them and then you'll be on your way when you get back to Dublin.' So that's what I did. I innocently sent back stuff to the *Irish Times*, but instead of running it with my by-line it was 'Our friend in Spain'. Then my friends from the *Irish Times* said, 'Thank you for the story. We had a few drinks at the Pearl Bar and toasted you!'

Then one of the news agencies sent her to meet Ernest Hemingway and ask him a rather silly question.

They didn't realise he'd been back to Spain a few times but the one question they gave to me was, 'Why have you come back to Spain for the first time since the Spanish Civil War? Franco is still in power. Nothing has changed.

Has something changed in your life?' And of course Hemingway looked at me as if I was quite crazy and said he was back in 1956 and 1953 on his way to Africa. So I paused and thought, what do I do now? Well, I'd better talk about what I know about, which was literary Ireland. Now, if that had been my uncle there'd have been a torrent of rage but with Hemingway he started asking me questions, like what other interviews have you done, whom was I seeing, where have I been. He told me to do things about Spain. And then he started giving me contacts and places I should go to . . .

In spite of Valerie's journalistic faux pas, Ernest picked her up tenderly like a gentle King Kong of American literature and placed her – figuratively speaking – on his shoulder. It seems that Valerie, in spite of herself, displayed a quality Ernest clearly admired. She had the makings of a good journalist. Ask the wrong question and you get the answer you weren't looking for – but maybe you get something even better than the right answer!

In Valerie, with her Irish background and Hemingway's fascination with all things rebellious, he instinctively knew a fellow spirit when he saw one.

Well, he said he would love to go to Ireland and he told me about James Joyce, and I admired Joyce because he was forbidden. When I went to England the first thing I did was buy *Ulysses* and I smuggled it back into Ireland, covered in a paper cover. He just loved that story. Hemingway had never been to Ireland and was always curious about it.

Valerie was quickly absorbed into the hurly-burly of Hemingway's helter-skelter life. She had to drink deep and long and be capable of keeping up into the early morning.

Spain was one long festival. We travelled north, south-east and west. There was always a party, always drinking . . .

I was fascinated by what was going on. I learned from Hemingway about the bullfight and about literature, it was all completely new to me. Nothing in my background prepared me for this. I was fascinated and didn't mind staying up listening to the stories. Someone would say, 'How could you listen to another story he tells?' but somehow each telling was fresh; like being a child and every time you hear a story you say, 'Tell me again, tell me again.'

Like all great writers he sometimes appropriated other people's experiences and tooled them carefully into gripping fiction.

Many of his stories were true stories about what had happened to him or his friends. And his friends sounded larger than life. I would meet them, including one Major General Buck Lanham. You know, 'BUCK LANHAM' – you have this image of someone rather large and forceful like Hemingway, and he turned out to be very small and timid and I just couldn't get over that – and other people where he built them up until they were fictional characters. There were always heroes and villains – his friends were the heroes, and the villains were the ones who hadn't measured up over the years. He had this wide cast of characters and they kept cropping up in his stories. For me, at that time, they were just names. Later I met a number of the people but many others were already dead by then. It was fascinating, constant entertainment.

Part of it was genius but part of it was plying his trade. He always called writing his trade and he did it, honed it, finely sharpened it. It was not an accident that he was such a good writer.

Hemingway was absolutely dedicated and competitive,

too. He wanted to be the best writer and often he felt that he was the best writer living at the time.

As Valerie observed, for Hemingway writing wasn't something you did after four hours in an opium hammock. At the Hemingway School of Writing you wrote with a cocked rifle and a loaded quill.

Writing was his weapon (when someone crossed swords with him) – he would either write a letter to the person and never send it, or do a fictional or actual account of the thing and put it in an envelope and seal it, 'private and confidential'. One image I have of Hemingway – when he's agitated, he gets into a boxer's stance, and that I think gives people pause not to go on with what they're doing. If Ernest started to shadow box then you retreated from whatever you were doing.

Valerie accompanied Hemingway on one of his famed bull-fighting tours of Spain. He wanted to formalise their relationship by taking her on as his assistant, but Valerie wasn't the kind of girl to say yes to any passing American literary giant, so she took some persuading.

Everybody in the *cuadrilla* [the group of friends] was moving down to Malaga for his birthday party. He asked me if I'd like to come. I didn't have the fare to Malaga and also had to work so I said, 'No, I'll be going back to Madrid.'

He said, 'Well, I'll pay your fare down,' and I still said no. I watched these people for a week and they were on a financial plane that I wasn't even aspiring to. I said to myself, 'No, enjoy what you've enjoyed and go back to Madrid.' It was the next day that he actually said jokingly to his friend Bill Davis, 'Don't you think the *cuadrilla* needs a secretary?' I was flabbergasted. In Ireland I was used to people jesting but this was no joke. 'Anyway,' he said, 'we can pay you two hundred and fifty dollars a month,' which was ten times what I was earning, so I had to say yes. And at the time it was just for July and August, for the bullfighting. He said, 'You'll learn far more about journalism working for me than you will staying in Madrid doing your interviews and things.' So there I was on my way. After working for him for three months he asked me, 'What would you call me in an emergency?' And then I realised I'd never addressed him by name; calling him Papa didn't seem right, and he hated being called Ernest. The Spanish called him Don Ernesto in Spain and some of the Cubans did too, but Ernest or Ernie, the name given to him by his mother, he was not that fond of.

My inclination was to call him Mr Hemingway but I just avoided calling him anything. But I would have called him Ernest.

It was summer 1959. In a pair of cars the group travelled across Spain, stopping only to watch bulls and to drink heavily. The writer and biographer A. E. Hotchner – 'Hotch' to those who knew him – was a close friend of Hemingway around this time, travelling with the party.* In a programme from BBC2s *Arena* documentary series shown in 1991, Hotchner remembered what it was like being on the road with a big cheese:

> We had a rented Ford which we got in Gibraltar. We loaded it up in Gibraltar, in particular because Ernest always felt you should have a wine sack in the front seat that was full of wine, ice that was at the ready, and in the back seat, the prime commodity we had purchased in Gibraltar was a huge wheel of Parmesan cheese. I was the occupant of the back seat with this wheel of cheese, and

---

* Writer of *Papa Hemingway*, widely regarded as the first creditable biography of Hemingway.

the summers in Spain get, as you know, pretty hot and the cheese got pretty hot. It was a long cheesy summer!

Valerie's great challenge was not holding her liquor but getting on the right side of Mrs Hemingway.

Mary was in the background. Even though she always made Ernest number one, she liked to have a billing that was coming close and she wasn't getting that, so Mary was sickly sweet and sarcastic to me. She would always say, 'I hope you're having a lovely time,' and you could tell that wasn't what she was hoping at all. In Spain, Mary was very disgruntled with Ernest, and that preceded my appearance on the scene; by September she was considering going home early, talking of divorce with him. It was in that period between when she left [Spain and returned to Cuba alone] and he left [Spain to join Mary in Cuba] that he asked me if I would come down to Cuba after the new year. 'I have to take care of Mary – she's my wife and if I've been good to one wife, I'll be good to another wife and I hope that once I get a divorce that you will marry me,' but I didn't for a moment believe it or even think that if he had said, 'Will you marry me?' and he were free, that I would have said yes. It was preposterous. That whole summer was quite preposterous. When I talked to a couple of friends they said if Ernest is infatuated with you, he'll get over it very quickly, so why not take the opportunity to go to Cuba and get as much out of it as you can?

Along with Spain, Africa and New York, Cuba was home to Hemingway. In 1959, the US backed Batista regime had been toppled and there was now a new leader in Havana, the communist Fidel Castro, who was forging links with the Soviet Union. Hemingway was returning to a changed Cuba.

We went there in January 1960. Castro had been in power since January 1959. There was initially an element of hope; even then there was a feeling of well-being. Castro was on the radio every day speaking for four to five hours, and they would *listen* with transistor radios as there wasn't any electricity. He was telling them how great their lives were going to be and so on. Generally, the people of Cuba had been ignored by Batista.

In the fifties, even before that, Cuba was full of casinos, artists and singers, a bit like Las Vegas. It was a holiday place, and even the Mob were in there. It had sunshine and was a beautiful setting. Castro clamped down on that. Hemingway's great friend Herbert Matthews had been in the mountains in the Sierra with Castro and was able to report for the *New York Times*. He got the scoop of Castro entering Havana and ousting Batista. Herbert talked a bit to me, saying that the *New York Times* was beginning to sub his pieces and not tell the truth. He'd asked for a new posting as a result. I overheard one conversation in which Hemingway spoke highly of Castro.

Hemingway was a Cuban hero because of his personality, not his writing. He was a great fisherman, sportsman and he enthused about Cuba.

Most Cubans wouldn't have read many of his books. A lot of them weren't even aware that he was a writer but they were aware that he was a VIP. Hemingway liked to keep it that way. 'This is where I come to write, and people don't bother me,' because they weren't concerned that he was a writer and they respected his privacy. He loved that.

Ernest was upbeat about Castro. His only interest was that Cuba should have a stable government so that he wouldn't be bothered. He was a great friend of the US ambassador Phil Bonsal, but he was friends with all the previous ambassadors and he was invited to all the cocktail parties. Ernest always kept close ties with the US and wanted to know what was going on, so that was one way of finding out.

Ernest Hemingway's Marlin Fishing Tournament fell within Castro's programme of nationalisation. The marlin, with its spear-like bill and tenacious character, is a worthy opponent for sport fishermen and requires an expensive boat and good equipment. Hemingway's competition was open to any Cuban who had acquired marlin-fishing boats and other gear left behind by rich, fleeing Americans.

At Hemingway's Marlin Fishing Tournament, Ernest was presenting the cup to Castro, who had won it. Because everything had been nationalised and all the sportsmen had left, the Cuban government had all these boats, so Castro happened to be about the only fisherman with the best equipment. Hemingway thought he'd won squarely. And they had a ten-minute photo op, and at the moment I went to shake hands with Castro and have my picture taken with him and Hemingway, these young girls broke through the rope and police came running after them and somebody whisked Castro away. My moment of glory was gone.

By now Mary and Valerie's relationship had thawed sufficiently for Valerie to feel that the Cuban house, La Finca, was her first real home. Hemingway even gave her one of his cats, which, if you're a fan of Hemingway, will have special significance. His love of cats was as famous as his books.

Ernest had a cat, Cristóbal Colón [Christopher Columbus]. Mary had a cat, Ambrosio Bierce, and then I was given my cat, which they called Pelusa, which means furry. But Ernest said it shouldn't be Pelusa. As it was St Patrick's Day, it had to be called Shamrock, and then that was shortened to Snocker [a pun, as snockered can mean inebriated]. I felt I was in with the whole household by that time. Mary had softened up and realised it was quite fun having a young person around.

I look back on Cuba as the happiest months of my life, except the cloud towards the end when Hemingway started to sink into this depression.

As history recalls, America's relationship with Cuba post-Batista soured very quickly and the presence of one of American literature's greatest stars on Cuban soil, minding his own business, tending to his writing and not bothering anyone, started to bother the American administration.

Phil Bonsal said that he'd been recalled and he wouldn't be coming back. He also said to Ernest, 'You need to leave! I've been given this message that you must leave as Washington's very unhappy about you continuing to live here in Cuba.' Most Americans had left the country. But, you see, with Hemingway his entire library was there; books given to him by the great authors. You couldn't take stuff out of Cuba. He was going to lose everything: animals, most of the staff – they were family!

This proved to be a turning point for Hemingway, and is a dark memory for Valerie.

He had confided in me that if he couldn't come back to Cuba and he couldn't write, that he would commit suicide. I was astounded because earlier on he'd told me about his father's suicide. Even though he really appeared to have affection for his father, he also scorned him and said, 'Suicide – it's the coward's way out.' I was just totally flabbergasted. He also said, 'You need to find yourself another job because I will not kill myself while you're around.'

[97]

Ernest was compelled by circumstances to leave his beloved Cuba, travelling with Valerie and Mary to New York. The gloom was lifted by trips to Madison Square Garden and the Metropolitan Museum of Art.

It was rather wonderful because he forgot about the suicide when we came to New York, and he wanted to show me the city. We went off to Toots Shor's bar [owned by Bernard 'Toots' Shor, whose Manhattan establishment was frequented by the biggest stars of the twentieth century] and there I met [baseball player] Mickey Mantle and [boxer] Gene Tunney and of course Toots himself, and we went to watch Archie Moore boxing in Madison Square Garden, one of his last fights. That was another thing I learned about Hemingway – he taught me to shoot and deep-sea fish, but every Friday [in Cuba] we watched the boxing. We followed the boxers and he had a betting pool. The male staff watched and he never allowed them to lose much money – it was just centavos [cents] – so because of watching Friday-night boxing with Hemingway, I knew all about Archie Moore, Gene Tunney and other boxers.

Then we went to the Metropolitan Museum. Ernest loved paintings. He said if he had not been a writer he'd have been painter. Well, I don't know whether you get the choice but he had a marvellous collection, all bought from the artists before they were famous – Miró, Braque . . . he loved the Winslow Homers.

During this time, Ernest was commissioned by *Life* magazine to write an article about two bullfighters who had locked horns over who was the better bullfighter. He returned to Spain to work on the article. Then news came from across the Atlantic that Ernest had collapsed at the bullring in Malaga.

I was disquieted when I heard about it so I flew back to Paris. He met me in Madrid at the train station and it was only a couple of weeks since I'd seen him last but I was amazed at how he'd changed . . . gaunt . . . he was haunted. Normally he never travelled alone, he always had someone with him, but I immediately noticed that there was fear in his voice. It was so unlike the year before. Instead of all the drinking, Ernest went to bed early, didn't come out to dinner, had room service . . . Then his friend A. E. Hotchner came to visit. He was back from London visiting [Hollywood actor] Gary Cooper, who was also a great friend of Hemingway, but another thing was that Coops, as he called him, had been diagnosed with cancer. Hotch was discussing making a movie of [Hemingway's] *Across the River and into the Trees*. Hotch was able to make everyone laugh, but this time Ernest wasn't laughing at his jokes.

It was time for him to go back to the States, and we saw him off in late October 1960. It was the last time I saw him and he said that he dearly wished the plane would crash so he wouldn't have to commit suicide. By this time I saw there was a person I couldn't reach, so reluctantly I went back to Ireland but I promised him I'd go to New York and I would be there if he needed to get in touch. I was on the staff of *Newsweek* magazine at the time and was visiting the Dunnes in Great Neck, Long Island – members of the family I had grown up with in the Summerhill Hotel – the first weekend of July 1961. At first there was something on the radio but they weren't sure. Then Mary telephoned me and asked if I'd come out to the funeral.

In a moment of need, prior to his suicide, Ernest wrote to Valerie asking her to come to him in Idaho, but the letter never reached her.

The very sad thing was that I didn't learn until forty years later that actually a week after he went to Idaho he wrote to me and asked me to get in touch. I never got the letter and later it was sold to a collector. It's now in the University of Virginia. I don't think it would have made any difference – he wouldn't have pulled himself out of it.

It was also very sad because it was another testimony that life isn't worth living because I'd said to him if you ever need me, I'll get in touch and I'll respond.

I thought I was hallucinating when I saw the letter on display at the Kennedy Library. I had removed any correspondence when I was going through Hemingway's papers, so when I saw something from him it was like something from the grave – here's something for me that I'd never seen before.

Ernest's wife Mary had become good friends with Valerie and asked her to work for the Hemingway estate. The first problem was that the estate was in Cuba and therefore officially the property of the Cuban state.

It was Castro who facilitated getting all of Mary's possessions and Ernest's papers out of Cuba. Castro would not help us overtly. He smiled and winked and said, 'We'll have to break a few laws here.' I thought he was very endearing.

Mary and Valerie were determined to get as much out of the Cuban house as possible, but with no diplomatic relations between America and Cuba, and a Soviet curator from St Petersburg sniffing round Ernest's personal belongings, the idea of getting anything off the island seemed hopeless.

Cuba had allied itself with Russia, and Russia had sent over experts from La Hermitage in St Petersburg to show Cuba how nationalisation takes place. This woman came out to categorise everything. Mary told her not to bother as 'I'm taking all of this back to the US', and the woman said, 'No, you're not.'

'Yes I am!' said Mary. 'I have the permission of El Jefe [Castro].'

'Castro has nothing to do with it. This property is nationalised and he has no say in it!'

Mary ignored the woman, and the moment the black Zil went down the driveway we took all the pictures off the wall, grabbed everything we could, covered our tracks, crated everything and went and sat on the dock of Havana Bay for a week until Mary saw a boat with an American flag. This boat was bringing back fishtails and shrimp from Argentina to Tampa and its refrigeration had broken down. Mary asked them if they would take the crates. At first they weren't interested, but when she produced a wad of American bills they agreed to take everything – millions of dollars of paintings and manuscripts. We realised we knew nothing of these people. We had no insurance.

But the ship got back to the US safely and – though she spent four years working for the Hemingway estate in the office of publisher Charles Scribner, cataloguing all Hemingway's papers for later presentation to the Kennedy Library in Boston, where they now reside – Valerie's close relations with the Hemingways appeared to be over.

Except they weren't. At Ernest's funeral she met Hemingway's son Greg, whose mother was Hemingway's second wife Pauline Pfeiffer.

I'd never met him before and I really knew nothing about him because his name wasn't allowed to be mentioned.

Valerie soon formed a close friendship with Greg and in 1966 she married him, becoming his third wife.

After we were married, Greg would never allow his father's name to be mentioned in the house. Our seven-year-old son came home from school one day and said, 'Is it true my grandfather was a great writer?' And it was only then I realised how we had never discussed Ernest in front of the children. That's how it was with the father and son.

I never saw the two in the same picture, as it were.

It's true that Greg had been his favourite son and he really tried so hard to emulate and be loved by his father, but from early on Greg had a tendency to cross-dress. This was not understood. I mean, I didn't understand him and I was married to him for a couple of years before I had any clue. Mysterious things were happening. I thought maybe he had a girlfriend or something. This, I think, was the unspoken bone of contention. Greg felt he was not understood by either of his parents.

It wasn't something he wished to be [a man]. He said he had one tragic flaw and that with all the good fortune in his life, this always came back to destroy whatever he built. He became a doctor but was always worried his secret life would be found out. Ernest had no understanding, nor his mum Pauline. It would have been dealt with by having to stop doing it.

The final break with his dad came after his mum died. Greg had been arrested in LA for using a women's bathroom and Pauline had rushed out. She had dual sympathies: to get him out of the mess and to avoid embarrassing Ernest. She called Ernest. They argued, with Ernest saying, 'You brought him up badly,' and then she died suddenly of an aneurysm. Greg became a doctor to find out why his mother died and it was way too late when he discovered that this is something that would have happened whatever. He told Ernest, 'You killed my mother!' because Ernest had yelled at her on the phone. Ernest retorted, 'You killed her; you were the cause of the incident we were arguing about,' and they never resolved that. In those days people didn't talk about this kind of behaviour. The final break with his dad came after his mum died.

In spite of these challenges Greg fathered four children with Valerie.

The children loved Greg and remember him very fondly. With the children he was more like an uncle than a dad, but he suffered from manic depression – bipolar – and he cross-dressed. I never saw him in that state early on in our marriage and it didn't affect the children while they were growing up but, as the years went on, he became more and more ill and because he was a doctor it was impossible to get him to see a doctor for help. Eventually we divorced because it became an impossibility to live with him. My youngest was seventeen when we divorced so they had him around most of their childhood.

Valerie continues to write as a journalist and now lives in Montana. Her memoir *Running with Bulls* was published in 2005.

6

I Was Les Dawson's Gag Writer

> He was full of fun. Not twisted in any way, just loving the
> fact that he'd found this great gift for comedy, and that he
> could share it with people he liked and make things that
> made other people laugh.

Writer David Nobbs (*The Two Ronnies, The Fall and Rise of
Reginald Perrin, A Bit of a Do, Going Gently, The Maltby Collection*)
first met up with comedian Les Dawson in the early seventies
when he became a script editor for him.

Les Dawson had an original comic persona: an expressive,
gurn-making face, with dog-hanging jaw, possibly the result of
a boxing injury. He was intelligent and quick-witted, with a
northern English *Weltschmerz* and a perfect club comic's deliv-
ery of deadpan one-liners which carried with them an additional emotional and melancholic charge, making him a great
insightful humorist in the body of a clown. He was largely con-
fined in his early years to the northern club circuit, carving
out a living as a club pianist and comedian. As well as being a
pianist he was also a prodigious writer (and reader) of books,
publishing many titles, and later brought musical comedy into
his act, including the Victor Borge-inspired performances of
classical pieces such as Beethoven's 'Moonlight Sonata', during
which he played wrong notes, increasing their number until
they became a cascade of dissonance. Of course, they weren't
just wrong notes but funny wrong notes. Les's particular bum
notes in these well-known pieces were comically inspired.
While his books were never quite as successful as his televi-

sion work, they showed he had poetic gifts and literary knowledge. His prose often spoofed popular literary styles – *Blade and the Passion, Come Back with the Wind, The Spy Who Came, Hitler Was My Mother-in-Law* or *Well Fared, My Lovely*. He was also a furiously active note-taker, writing poetry and comic ideas alongside an open-hearted diary of events in his life, since published as *Les Dawson's Secret Notebooks*.

Dawson's first break came on the talent show *Opportunity Knocks* in 1967. He made a string of TV appearances in the sixties and seventies, each showcasing his trademark style – the face of a bored jester with the stealthy intellect of an alternative comedian. At times it appeared he was ridiculing the variety and club roots he had come from. Perhaps he was. Nowhere was this more apparent than on his hosting of *Blankety Blank*, facing a panel of many of his colleagues and mentors – Barry Cryer, Danny La Rue and Kenny Everett, to name a few. He would spar with them, sometimes with scripted jokes, sometimes with pure improvisation, but always carrying utterly memorable facial expressions, coupled with a faux-jaded mordancy that created a unique comic tension for Saturday-night television entertainment, the like of which would not be seen again until Michael Barrymore started flying off script with improvised mayhem in *Strike It Lucky*. Les Dawson's brilliant style was almost too subversive for its time. It was also unmissable because of that. John Cleese was a big fan.*

---

* Cleese frequently appeared in many editions of Dawson's sketch show *Sez Les*. Here is a YouTube clip in which Les's character is being interviewed for a job in accounting. It dates from 1971 and stars Cleese, Dawson and Gordon Kaye: youtube.com/watch?v=tbd4px8tKao.

This is another sketch featuring Cleese and Dawson: youtube.com/watch?v=fz5ZbDaXG4M&feature=related.

And here is a joke from his opening monologue on *Blankety Blank*: youtube.com/watch?v=gLe1_pnxKV4&feature=related.

One of his edgiest and most popular shows was Yorkshire Television's *Sez Lez*, which ran on Saturday nights from 1969 to 1976. Cissie Braithwaite and Ada Shufflebotham, two nosy old women – played by himself and Roy Barraclough – were instantly memorable, and based on the demonstrative visual language of Mancunian factory workers trying to communicate gossip over the noise of machinery. *Sez Lez*, unusual for its sexy edge at the time, was a major hit.

David Nobbs was one of Les Dawson's key gag and sketch writers during this period.

*

I was born in Orpington, Kent, and I went to school in a kindergarten in Wiltshire during the war which was run by a Miss Kinder, which is why I thought it was called a kindergarten. And when some other child said that they were in a kindergarten run by a Miss Brown, I said, 'No, that's a browngarten.'

Then I went to a prep school, long defunct, in Bickley, Kent, and then boarding school at Marlborough. It was a very good school, and I left knowing quite a bit, which I've steadily forgotten over the long years that followed.

David was inspired to write initially by the works of Evelyn Waugh.

I read a book by Evelyn Waugh. I think *Decline and Fall* was the first one. The dialogue just spoke to me and I thought I would like to be able to do that sort of thing. I wrote ridiculous ideas for books, mainly about badgers, when I was about nine. And suddenly it came to me: I want to be funny.

There was a master who encouraged me in a literary society, but right at the end, when I was just about eighteen and just before I left, the bug began to really kick in.

I did write one article. I reviewed the Cadet Corps Day, and I remember perhaps my first joke in print: 'As we marched down Marlborough High Street, reputedly the widest high street in Marlborough.'

David reluctantly found himself in the school cadets.

I think you probably had to be in those days. And I was on to national service, you see. We went around with simulated guns as far as I remember. We carried things which were supposed to be guns. We may have fired off blanks, I don't really remember. Lots of people came round and said, 'You, you and you are dead. You, you and you aren't.' I hated every minute of it.

I left school in 1953. My heroes were, very largely, sportsmen at that stage, including Len Hutton, who was my great hero. I loved cricket, and still do. And I was beginning to enjoy the humorous writing of P. G. Wodehouse, Evelyn Waugh, as I said, and so on.

You can't be in the cadets and not play cricket.

I played, not very well, but with enthusiasm, and when I went to university I captained a team which played without great seriousness against the villages, which I thoroughly enjoyed.

Cricket was important to me at that stage of my life. I did some sailing. I was much more of an outdoor person than I later became. But still, the ambition was there now to be a writer.

My first writing job after I left university was as a reporter on the *Sheffield Star*. I was then moved to the Rotherham office; they explained to me that as it was smaller this was a kind of promotion. That didn't fool me for a moment, and I was one of the world's worst journalists ever, I should think.

I did this for about eighteen months and wrote my first novel in the evenings. There were only two kinds of evening: evenings when I sat in my digs and wrote, and evenings when I sat in a pub and drank. And that was my life.

My novel was called *The Itinerant Lodger*. It was [very] sort of influenced by the world of Theatre of the Absurd, and Ionesco and N. F. Simpson and so on. It was kind of a contradiction in terms in the title, which was the kind of absurdity that I was revelling in.

I was very much influenced by stage writers, and Harold Pinter when he came along as well. And Beckett. All these spoke to me very directly, I felt, but somehow never got translated into my doing much in the theatre myself. I turned to books, and then got involved in *That Was the Week That Was*, which set me off on ten or more years of writing for various comedians. That led through to all the Frost programmes, and that led through to *The Two Ronnies*. I wrote for Ken Dodd, Tommy Cooper and Frankie Howerd. I must be one of the very few people ever to turn down the annual dinner of the St John's College, Cambridge, Classical Society with the explanation that I was in the studio with Jimmy Tarbuck.

Of course, now that would be seen as incredibly cool.

Well, the word 'cool' hadn't really entered our vocabulary at that stage. Certainly nowadays, yes. A bit of street-cred there perhaps, more so than knowing all about Cicero.

Writing comedy is a very challenging occupation, as anyone who does it for a living will tell you, but writing comedy for other comedians is even more challenging.

It's a strange life writing for comedians. You have to write in the style of the particular comedian most of the time, and Frankie Howerd posed a particular problem because he had a very unusual speech pattern. I remember I was wrestling with this, and I had to do it out loud. So there I was in my study, talking – he was the only comedian I had to talk out loud to myself to get the rhythm – and the children were in the next room making tea with some school friends. One of them came in and said, 'Look, could you be a bit more quiet? It's really embarrassing – our friends think you're a loony.'

So I went out. I lived on a common in North London. I went out and walked across the common, relating the lines, getting the rhythm and then rushing back in and writing a bit down. But the second time I was out there, as I was talking I noticed a police car going along alongside me. Three policemen stopped, got out, came over to me and said, 'And what do you think you're doing?' My reply – 'Writing for Frankie Howerd' – didn't seem very convincing. I had no paper, I had no pen. They looked at me very suspiciously.

Luckily I had on my person, in my wallet, a membership card for the Writers' Guild of Great Britain. I showed them this, and they looked at it and realised that I was just a mad writer, and they said, 'Terribly sorry, sir, but we have had rumours of an escaped lunatic in the area.'

So when did David first hear about Les Dawson?

Some time in the early seventies I took a job as a script editor at Yorkshire Television for a year. I enjoyed it, but nothing great came of it until John Duncan, head of comedy at Yorkshire, suggested that I might become script editor for a new series of shows with Les Dawson.

Les had been doing quite a lot of shows. I already knew

that I liked his work, but I hadn't studied him with any particular interest, and I didn't realise that this was going to lead to sixty-eight shows with Les. For all the other things I've done, they remain one of the great highlights for me of my life.

I have to confess now that the title 'I Was Les Dawson's Gag Writer' is perhaps not one hundred per cent true – but in modern Britain what is one hundred per cent true? – because Les wrote his own monologues. We weren't allowed to touch his monologues, and we wouldn't have wanted to. They were absolute gems.

I remember when I went to see Les, to see one of his old-style shows and to be introduced to him and all that sort of thing, the very first thing he was talking about was a visit to the all-night windmill. The idea of an all-night windmill is a sort of wonderfully bizarre idea that Les just threw out. He was very inventive, very witty, very talented and in all respects except one a very generous man.

Our series was called *Sez Les*. I got my great friend Barry Cryer in, and he and I did probably the bulk of the writing. There was another friend too, Peter Vincent. A young man called John Hudson appeared on the scene and wrote lovely sketches until he decided to give up writing and go into a more conventional career and get married. Having seen us at work, he can't have been that impressed or something, I don't know.

We created a show which was at first full of very, very quick-firing gags with lots and lots of running characters. There was Cosmo Smallpiece, the sex-obsessed man in horn-rimmed spectacles who was hooked off stage every time he got more and more to the point of getting unacceptably filthy. Probably today this would be regarded as unacceptable in the age of worry about paedophilia and perverts of every kind. Dawson Welles, that's sort of self-explanatory – Les as Orson Welles was wonderful. Buster Gut, the world's oldest and worst stuntman, and a marvellous David Attenborough impression, always in a whisper, in the presence of animals doing various strange things. And we'd just roll these off, and everybody on the show was able to contribute ideas and write little sketches, and there was a wonderful feeling to it.

Les Dawson seemed to be more intrigued by telling stories than gags; he seemed to be a natural storyteller in a way – almost more feminine than masculine.

I think in a way Les was both masculine and feminine at the same time. I mean, he was a real heavy-drinking northerner, but he also had a sensitivity. And incidentally, he loved playing women. His Cissie and Ada things with Roy Barraclough were absolute gems, mostly not written by us – that was the other bit that he usually wrote – and they were a tribute to a whole range of music-hall comedians that he liked, Norman Evans's 'Over the Garden Wall' being one of them. But Les was always very happy to do new things, and that was the great thing. You didn't have to write every sketch in Les Dawson's style. We even did a few sketches with John Cleese, who was a great admirer of Les.

Barry and I managed to write a sketch based on *Hamlet* which did not get one single laugh when starring Les Dawson and John Cleese. I mean, that's pretty fearsome, isn't it? But most of our stuff went down very well and Les was a joy to work for.

Dawson was quite clear about working stuff out technically, but as a viewer myself, some of the skits appeared to be improvised.

I think Les distinguished very, very well which bits of the show you could improvise and in which bits of the show you had to stick to the script. He was marvellous at sticking to a well-written script. He didn't diverge from it because he had a great sense of timing and structure and he knew how a joke should work. I think the most exciting thing for me was the way he would take on any physical role. A lot of comedians would say, 'I don't have to do this to get laughs.'

For instance, my favourite that Barry and I did was Jock Cousteau, the world's leading underwater bagpiper. Les did it live in front of a studio audience, dressed up in a kilt; went, playing the bagpipes, up a ladder and down into a tank of water until he was utterly and totally submerged and all you could hear were bubbles. I mean, it was just so funny.

And all these other comedians, I don't think you'd have dared suggest it to them even, because they'd have looked at you as if you were mad, going, 'I don't have to do this.' Les never minded that sort of thing.

David was by then an established novelist, and I wondered whether Les ever discussed his own writing with him.

He certainly didn't come to me for advice. He was very proud of the novels that he wrote. I think he was aware that he was learning, but he was very determined to learn and to improve as a writer. At his memorial service at Westminster Abbey, there were extracts of a new novel which was almost mystical in its intentions, and there's no doubt that he took this side seriously. I don't know how good he would have turned out to be, to be honest.

I think in a way it's a slight shame that, like so many people, he sensed that there's something more rewarding than comedy, something better than comedy. Whereas I think if you happen to have that rare gift of making people laugh, you should be able to express all your other thoughts through comedy.

Did David read any of Les's novels?

I did, and I thought they showed his inexperience of the novel form in a way, but they were still readable because Les was talented. I think they would have improved enormously. I mean, if I look at my early novels – I did read my second novel *Ostrich Country* a few years ago. I started off reading it thinking, 'God, this is great. This is terrific.' As I did it, you've got to think it's good. I lost interest halfway through, and didn't even bother to get to the end to find out what happened. And you might think I knew what happened because I wrote it, but I'd forgotten.

I only make that point to show that – unless you're very, very lucky and your writing comes to you sort of fully fledged – most people have to work up to find their true abilities and voice. And Les was doing that in his writing and was cut short before he found it, really.

Was Dawson respectful of David's public-school background? Was that an area of humorous conflict? They did have something in common however; it was called national service.

From the public school and before Cambridge I did two years as a foot-slugger in the Royal Signals, and after Cambridge I did my year and a half in the thick of it in Sheffield and Rotherham on the *Sheffield Star*, so my life was not that of a socialite in many of its aspects. I was very much a lover of the northern working-class life that I'd experienced when I was on the paper, so I don't remember any real conflict of that kind at all.

National service did have a uniting quality, but I still think it was something that cannot work successfully unless you have really useful things for people to do. I could talk to you for hours about the absurdities of my national service, the complete time-wasting. The fact is that a whole generation learned how to skive, and put skiving into practice in the factories afterwards.

Early in his career Dawson went to Paris with the sole objective of becoming a famous writer. He gave himself ten days.

He did talk about the Paris trip, and he made it, like he made everything, into a comic routine. But there was affection for the image, and for the absurdity. He was able to laugh at himself, he was able to see how in the long line of would-be Parisian intellectuals this strange-looking, gurning figure did not perhaps quite sit entirely comfortably, and he loved the thought of that.

He would talk to us about books he'd read, mainly just quoting lines that he'd particularly liked. Sitting with him was always fun, because there was always humour. And unlike many comedians he relished being topped. If he told a funny gag and you topped it, he roared, and he slapped his side and he was delighted for you and with you. That's rare.

Dawson's writing drew some attention from contemporary drama writers, as David recalls.

There were attempts made to sort of move Les up, with sitcom-type things written by Simpson and Galton, and Alan Plater. And great though those writers undoubtedly are, Barry [Cryer] and I felt slightly miffed that they didn't come to us to take him a little bit further, because we knew him so well. We never got that opportunity, which I do regret, because I think of all the comedians I worked for he became the one I admired the most and it would have been lovely to go further.

He moved to the BBC, partly I think because people at Yorkshire Television wanted to make Yorkshire Television more respectable. Their drama was always national rather than regional and I think they didn't want the idea of flat-capped comedians; they wanted something more sophisticated. So Les went to the BBC and Meg, his wife, fell seriously ill. This was why he stopped doing his new entertainment shows and went on to *Blankety Blank*, which of course was terribly easy for him – he could do it virtually in his sleep. But it meant that the last part of his career, we would look back now and say was a disappointment. I think that is due entirely to his untimely death. I think that ways would have been found of finding a great niche for him somewhere, maybe in narrative form.

Did he have the abilities to be an actor?

He had his limitations – most actors have their limitations – but they're outweighed by his strengths. I think he could move you and make you laugh at the same time. I think he could touch you in all sorts of ways.

I wouldn't say he was a great intellectual or a sort of mental genius or anything, but there's a quality there that could rise to great heights when pointed in the right direction.

Although no deep friendship emerged between them, the day-to-day joy of writing jokes and coming up with funny material created a unique bond in itself.

I think he became a friend to me and Barry, and the whole team for a while, but Les lived for the day to a certain extent. At the end of it all, we felt we were great friends.

We'd shared lots of meals out together; we'd even gone to a topless bar together, which we all laughed about the next day. I mean, Les just thought it was absurd, as he thought most things were absurd.

He said, 'I'll see you all at the BBC,' and he never did. We felt he'd let us down then, but I don't feel that now. I understand now. The BBC would have said, 'Look, you need someone new, you've moved, you've got to do something completely different.' And quite rightly, probably; he went into new areas and our role, I think, looking back on it, would have been to come in again with fresh ideas, maybe five years later, but of course by then he was gone.

So in the end we drifted apart, really, but just because that's the nature of showbiz, when you're working with people. While we worked with him he was definitely a friend. He didn't go off at six o'clock in his car. He stayed with us, ate with us, drank with us a lot of the time, and we had a lot of fun.

I think the idea that all comedians are driven by self-loathing, or even by sadness, is a myth. Well, it's not a myth – many comedians are. But not all.

I don't think he had a lot of sadness apart from things like Meg's illness and death, the things that anybody would be sad about. He was full of fun. Not twisted in any way, just loving the fact that he'd found this great gift for comedy, and that he could share it with people he liked and make things that made other people laugh; quite simple at heart really.

Blankety Blank, **Dawson's last major television show, worked because he was satirising the very form that had made him a star.**

I think whatever Les had done, there would have been an

element of affectionate satire in it, so I think he would not have taken that role particularly seriously.

He was quite near the knuckle at times. Very near the knuckle – as near the knuckle as you need to go. I think it's much funnier to be near the knuckle than to be utterly and totally outspoken. You've got nowhere to go. My great friend Alan Plater says that when you've said 'I love you', there's no further story to be told. And when you've used every swear word in the book and made jokes about every kind of physical ailment and things, there's nothing left to do. You've sort of blown it in my opinion.

Les moved to the BBC and this was the end of the road. We weren't asked to write for him again. I think in time, had he lived, we might have been. I'm sure, for all my other commitments and my other loves in my career, I would have said yes.

I wondered what Les had made of *The Fall and Rise of Reginald Perrin*.

I think he admired it. He was a generous man, you see; he was never worried if you had successes. I think he was delighted. And he knew that I wasn't the sort to go round boasting about it. I remember him being impressed by it.

It's clear that Les Dawson would have been superb in one of David's sitcom creations.

I don't even want to think about it because it suddenly seems like a lost opportunity. Now here I am with all my experience – if Les was here, what could we do for him, you know?

Les Dawson died of a heart attack on 10 June 1993 following a check-up at Whalley Range Hospital in Manchester.

I don't think I was utterly surprised, because he did sort of live in the fast lane. He was a big drinker, so there were a lot of late nights and early mornings. I think he punished his body. So in that sense, I wasn't utterly surprised, but the actual facts of it, which I don't remember in detail, seemed to suggest that it was more of a sudden medical problem relating to an illness that would otherwise have been happily cured. So I don't think it was inevitable at all.

David is a prolific writer of novels and sitcoms. Indeed, even Reggie Perrin has returned, with Martin Clunes in the lead role. I wondered if Les's comic glow had any impact on David's writing style.

There's perhaps a fulsomeness of language and a relish of words which was heightened by working with him. I think that it's very difficult for me to say what impacts on my style. If you're self-conscious about it, it doesn't come out right. I know that when writing a book, I absolutely refuse to have any connection whatsoever with Dylan Thomas, because I'm half Welsh and it will come out as a Welsh torrent if I'm not careful. So, no Dylan Thomas. And one of my publishers said to me, 'David, you're reading too much Nabokov, because you're getting a bit Nabokov, you see.'

After he and Dawson parted company, David continued to write comedy for many TV talents through the seventies.

This was a period when things were developing for me very fast. *The Two Ronnies* – that carried on throughout all this in its calm, professional, ordered and extremely enjoyable way, without the same excitement perhaps, but just as good an end product.

And of course *Reginald Perrin* changed my life. I was now

able to do what I wanted to do. Those three series still bring me royalties from all over the place.

The Fall and Rise of Reginald Perrin, first screened by the BBC in 1976, was an astonishing piece of work. At the time we had Monty Python bringing us absurdist comic sketches, and Nobbs had himself been profoundly influenced by the work of N. F. Simpson. With *Reginald Perrin* he successfully combined the subversive and absurd into a cleverly disguised BBC sitcom set in suburbia. It was a massive success. It was also very funny.

When I look back on my life, the significance of the Frost era cannot be overstated, because I sat at a table with the five Monty Python boys making jokes and suggestions for a programme. And then they went off to do their wonderful surreal stuff. I was really churning out gags for comedians who, as I said earlier, have their own style.

With Les, I got nearer to being able to do the kind of thing that they [Monty Python] were doing. In my own work, clearly this was what I wanted to do – there is this absurdist element in my writing.

I had a wonderful time. The only thing I must say about *Reginald Perrin* is that when it was on *Mastermind*, and one woman had as her special subject the scripts and books of *Reginald Perrin*, everybody was in fits of laughter because one of the questions on dear old serious *Mastermind* was: when Reggie had a smelling contest of aerosols etc., what smell did he say all the things reminded him of? And the answer was a Bolivian unicyclist's jockstrap. Now, this is not the sort of thing you usually get on *Mastermind*. Everybody was in hysterics, but the funniest thing about it all was that there were seventeen questions. This woman scored seventeen; I got eight.

7

I Was Tina Turner's White Dancer

Girl, you're not just white, you're *real* white; you got that
blonde hair and those blue eyes.

Tina Turner remains unique amongst R'n'B singers. Her initial
stage pairing with husband Ike produced one of the most
electrifying live acts of the sixties, melding soul with sex in a
way even Prince would shrink from. If you don't believe me
watch *Gimme Shelter*, the Maysles brothers' 1970 documentary film of the Rolling Stones's 1969 tour, and look out for
the clip of Tina singing 'I've Been Loving You Too Long', filmed
at Madison Square Garden. This was as close a singer could get
to an orgasm onstage without being arrested.

Behind the scenes, the Turners' relationship was a violent
and abusive one. After separating, Ike released two poorly
received albums and later did prison time for drugs and weap-
ons offences. Tina carried on with her recording career and
live work. She was still a presence in the seventies, albeit one
with a lower profile than she'd had in the sixties with Ike, but
the arrival of eighties group BEF (British Electric Foundation),
their production of 'Let's Stay Together' and her appearance
on Channel 4's *The Tube* in 1983 suddenly introduced her to a
new and appreciative audience. The spectacle of Live Aid and
the explosion of corporate rock in the mid-eighties propelled
her to a level of success both onstage and on disc that remains
astonishing.

A defining part of Tina Turner's universal appeal was her
sassy stagecraft and choreography, in particular her use of

black and white dancers. Echoing Sly and the Family Stone's racially diversified group of ten years earlier, Tina opted for a set of two backing singers/dancers onstage with her during many of her eighties and nineties tours: Lejune Richardson was black; Ann Behringer white.

Ann was born into a liberal, slightly WASPy New England family and imbued with a set of ideals that everybody was equal regardless of tribe, colour, religion or orientation. Ann was also a keen dancer from a very early age — almost, it seems, since she could walk.

*

I wanted to be a dancer since I was a little girl. I couldn't stop dancing. I danced to *Hullabaloo* and *Shindig, American Bandstand*. I always got popular feedback from parents and relatives on my dancing. So it was a good place for me to start.

My first dance hero was José Greco. I was five years old and he was a famous flamenco dancer. I still, to this day when I see that kind of dancing and music, I just go crazy. I love it. In fact, I can imitate it right now!

I studied dance very late in my life. I was eighteen years old. I was told by all my teachers and family I should try acting, as it wasn't too late for that, but I was absolutely determined to become a dancer and eventually I did, because by the time I was twenty-four I was a full-time professional.

Ann's dance career began in 1967 with a progressive, theatrical, American punk-rock group who pushed the taste limit onstage to number eleven with some of their performances. These were the godfathers of art-house American punk: the Tubes.

I danced with the Tubes. I met them when I was fifteen in 1967 in Phoenix, Arizona, before they were known as the Tubes. I would just dance and they incorporated me into their show. I was Madame Butterfly with her butterfly girls and there were all these other girls that would follow me. I was like a whirling dervish. I just didn't stop, I just kept moving. I had this really long hair and I would swing it all around. Those are the first people I danced with. I danced with a lot of rock 'n' roll bands, danced in Vegas and danced on some TV shows, one of which was called *Midnight Special*, in the seventies.

Like *Oh! Calcutta!* meeting the New York Dolls in Little China, the Tubes were at times unpredictable, and way out in front of the dark American punk subculture to come.

People didn't get them. They wanted me to join the band, and I think I'd be dead if I had. There was so much drug-taking and drinking. I knew intuitively not to join that band.

As it turned out, that was probably a wise choice, but the experience simply confirmed Ann's desire to dance and improve the style she most enjoyed.

My best way of dancing is improvised. It was my most comfortable place. I studied jazz, African, ballet – a lot of ballet, because that's the core in dance. Now I still do hip-hop. I still take class at least four times a week. I will never stop dancing!

I wanted to learn technique, to improve, with more freedom. I knew that if I learned how to do a turn technically, I could do a turn better.

It was rock rather than ballet that inspired her dancing.

From the very beginning it's been as if the music goes through my body. I can remember watching John Mayall's Bluesbreakers when he had Eric Clapton playing guitar. I literally popped out of my chair. I couldn't even sit down. If I hear music in a store and it's a song I like, I love to move. It's hard not to move. It's like a tic.

Ann gained more experience dancing with various outfits and groups. Then she received a call from Tina Turner's choreographer, Toni Basil.

Tina needed another white dancer. Toni Basil was asked to put out a call to a dancer who she thought would be good. I'd worked with Toni on one of her shows. We had a blast. I got the call.

It was a private audition, there were ten or twenty of us who all came over to Tina's house one at a time.

Ann had been given a tape containing songs to learn.

Tina was dressed in a T-shirt and the first thing she asked was, 'Can you sing?' And so I sang and she said, '*Wow*, you can really sing!' Then she had me dance and she said, 'Well, your dancing needs work!' [*Laughs*] It was a shock! I listened. I was fine with it. Tina Turner was never taught to dance formally. She was a street dancer. All her movements go back to Ike. She would say, 'Girl, it's a feel thing.'

A week later they called me. I came in, she sat me down and said, 'Would you like to have this job?' and I said, 'Yeah!' I'm twenty-seven years old and I was like, 'Oh my God, I can't believe I'm going to dance with somebody I idolise.' When I saw her on TV at fifteen years old – saw this black woman with these big legs, butt and everything shaking – I thought, 'Woah, this is me, this is me!' I picked up on that energy and I related to it.

[128]

Anyway, she said, 'You want the job?'

'Yeah!'

'Great, you got it!'

'But there are two things I won't do.' And she looked at me like, 'Oh no, oh God, she's already a trouble-maker.' I said, 'I won't cut my hair,' and I had hair past my waist.

'Oh, good, don't cut your hair, don't cut it an inch, don't cut it one bit!'

'I won't drink or use, no matter what!'

And she said, 'Great!' Like . . . no problem! And that was it. I got the job!

At the time, Ann had recently overcome a long addiction to drink and drugs. Had she found it difficult to stay clean during physically demanding and emotionally overwhelming global tours?

It wasn't a nightmare. What was great about it was that first of all I was dancing with a dream come true, I was dancing with Tina Turner. I idolised her and it offered a contained environment. What's good about the road is that your whole day, the whole twenty-four hours, is set out for you. You live in a contained group, in a bus or a plane, you have a schedule, a sound check, you have the show, you have to go to bed, and I thrived in that kind of environment. I think it's actually what kept me sober, because the thought of using on the road, which came up all the time because I was still craving, you know, coke and things like that, the thought of losing that job was much more . . . I could not do it. I would not use. I would not lose that job, no way, so it kept me sober.

And there was another reason for Ann to fear a return to the bottle.

I come from a long line of female alcoholics. My great-grandmother, my grandmother and my mother died because of this disease. I knew something was wrong with me early on when somebody told me I was an alcoholic at the age of twenty-one. I knew that they were right. I did not know about Alcoholics Anonymous; I did not know that abstinence was the way to treat it. But I came to a point in my career when I was dancing in a movie called *Xanadu* [with Olivia Newton-John], and I knew that if I kept using and drinking, my career as a dancer was finished, and I had a choice to make. Somebody had told me about AA and I was really drawn to it, so I decided that the last day of this movie is the day I get sober. I just got sober. I never looked back. Twenty-nine years later I'm still sober because it was like a relief for me, like a ball and chain had been taken off my neck. I mean, I was using on the set in that movie. It was a very professional set. I did not see a lot of drug use there. It was closeted if it was there, but I was using up a storm.

Isolated and alone on the film, she hit a wall.

I had a friend tell me, 'This is what's wrong with you, this is what you need.' A guy I used with – he's a year more than me, he's still sober too – he took me to my first meeting. And I never looked back. It saved my life. Everything in my life is strictly a result of getting sober. I mean, I would have never made it to the Tina Turner audition; I would never have been able to do that job.

It's clear that after what Tina Turner had had to tolerate from her husband towards the end of their relationship – he made no secret of his prodigious use of cocaine – she'd have tolerated no more out-of-control substance abuse.

Oh, she was relieved that one of her people didn't have drug or alcohol problems, believe me. I mean, after Ike and all that went down with that!

Yeah . . . people said in the AA programme, 'Oh, you're gonna use, you're gonna relapse!' But my sponsor in the programme said, 'Go! Go!' [on the Tina Turner tour], and I worked the programme on the road.

This was 1979 and Ann was to stay as Turner's 'white' dancer right the way through to the Foreign Affair tour of the early nineties.

She didn't have any other dancers until after 1991. There was a break in there when she had no dancers, but when she wanted dancers she got us back.

In fact, Ann was with her for the best part of twelve years.

I got on with her really well, you know. I learned a lot from her. Lejune, Tina and I, we stayed close – we were like a unit. As things speeded up in her career, it got more fragmented, it got more intense for her, she had more interviews. There was more work to do.

The speeding up in Turner's career was due mostly to the arrival of her new manager, Roger Davis, and the hit eighties reworking of 'Let's Stay Together', the video of which shows Ann in performance. Davis turned her from a Vegas act into a global rock property.

Tina Turner was suddenly a born-again rock goddess, with a breathtaking show to match that Ann was almost born to be in.

I 'grew up' with Tina. I was somewhat immature when I got the job. I mean, I was a professional, but I really grew up with her. She taught me that I could do things in my

dancing that I wasn't aware I could until she pushed me.
She taught me really good lessons about the colour of my
skin. White folks take for granted they're white folks but
people of colour never ever take that for granted. They live
in a dual cultural reality, and she would say, 'Girl, you're
not just white. You're *real* white; you got that blonde hair
and those blue eyes.' She would say stuff like that and it
was a good lesson for me. It would really help me understand not to take it for granted that people . . . Just because
I was a liberal and believe that everybody's equal, it's not
necessarily so.

I feel she had to trust me over time to realise. One time
she said to me, 'You're white but you're really a high-yellow
heifer', which was a huge compliment.* Over the years it
wasn't about colour any more. She went through the sixties, riding in a bus, having to watch her back down in the
South, you know? Even when I started working with her in
the seventies we never went to the South.

**Tina was born in Tennessee, and she would often describe
what it was like for her growing up in America's South.**

She had a tough life, not just because she was black but
because she was from a mother who left and a father
who . . . I don't know . . . She had Ike, and what that was
like. The thing that struck me the most was what it was like
to be black in the South, and how dangerous it was, and
she would share some of that. Later, when she toured in the
Deep South they'd have to duck Rhonda – Tina's personal
assistant, who is white – below the windows of the tour
bus in certain towns, because they could not have a white
person travelling next to a black person.

* The term 'high yellow' is used to describe a light-skinned African
American.

Many African Americans have been conditioned by generations of enforced subservience to feel resentment towards whites. I wondered how Tina felt about playing to and entertaining a predominantly white audience, and whether that influenced her when she performed.

She was always aware – completely and utterly aware. Anybody who is not white doesn't think about what colour they are. In the USA, though, it has changed radically. The whole hip-hop thing has mixed it up so much. My step-daughter's generation, they don't even think that way. But I was brought up to think like that. My mother said we are all equal, but I understand now that it was an ideal. It was not the truth.

In the early eighties, we went to South Africa during apartheid and Tina got a lot of flak for that, but the thing is we played to mixed crowds and we were a mixed band, and I think it was a good thing we went there.

Dancing with Tina Turner in front of thousands of people was a daunting, exhilarating experience.

I don't know how to describe it, except that it's one of the most intense experiences getting out there with a loud R'n'B band, the music, dancing and a hundred thousand people screaming at you – it's exhilarating, you know. You're adrenalised. Before I got onstage every night, I would be frozen. I would try to stretch out but the only thing that would get me ready for that crowd was, I would stand behind the stage – Tina was onstage already, we'd come on afterwards – and I would do a primal scream, three times, literally as loud as I could, and then I would go out there and hit it, because you have to hit up against all that energy, and then I'd swing my hair round.

According to Ann, in spite of having achieved so much and defined herself in such original terms as a solo performer, Turner's past continued to haunt her.

She was always afraid that Ike would turn up. She would always get agitated if there was a rumour that he was going to be at a show. When she left him he took more or less everything except her name, so he couldn't really get anything from her and he never was 'nice' like that, that I know of. Maybe he did turn up to concerts, but I was never aware of it. I know that she would get agitated when he was potentially in the audience.

Turner's independence from Ike and her astonishing solo career did not come without bruises and experience. Ann often found her a source of great wisdom and encouragement.

She said I should sing more. I did back-ups [backing singing] with her on one of the shows. I loved that. I watched her. She's incredibly professional. She works no matter what she feels like. Because she would say, 'Oh, you're sick. I guess you can't get onstage!' I got onstage, sick as a dog. I never missed a show because I was never going to have her say, 'Oh, you poor thing.' She was tough and I wanted to be tough too.

I used to think that I'd like to be like Tina Turner – well, not her directly, you know, but Madonna or something like that. I can remember standing behind her as a back-up singer/dancer and watching her and thinking, 'I am so glad I am doing back-up.' I got over that onstage. The responsibility on a star singer is beyond words. It's worse for her now and has been for a long time. We couldn't be in a restaurant without somebody coming up and bugging us – that's while we were eating! There was no privacy –

ever – you know. I was very happy to be her back-up singer and dancer.

Perhaps because of this realisation, Ann decided during one of the breaks from touring to pursue another direction. It was 1990.

We had four years off the road and I decided to go back to school because I thought, 'What do I want to be?' I did not want to be a choreographer. I did not want to teach dance. I love to dance. I could have been a choreographer because I can choreograph. I really wanted to start using my mind. I had a bad childhood. I went to five high schools but I realised I had a brain. Tina used to say, 'Girl, you got a brain in there, you're always reading and stuff,' and she was right. I do have a brain and I went back to school and started psychology and became a therapist.

Having stopped drinking just before joining Turner's entourage, Ann rejoined it for the What's Love tour in 1993, this time as a fledgling therapist and still one of the 'dry' members of the band. Did she become an evangelist for an alcohol-free lifestyle?

It was around me all the time, not that everybody was doing it. It was there, though, and there were a couple of people I tried to get sober, and they're dead because of the disease and they died young, and died, definitely, because of drugs and alcohol.

Tina Turner had converted to Nichiren Shoshu Buddhism after leaving Ike in the seventies.

I went to meetings all over the world, and sometimes when Tina and Lejune would chant [Lejune was also a Buddhist] I would sit in with them. I used to chant with them.

With Tina and Lejune chanting the Gohonzon and Ann following the twelve-steps programme, a casual observer might be
forgiven for thinking this was less a rock 'n' roll lifestyle, more
a philosophical sleepover. Ann was now beginning to feel a
strong desire to do something different.

The show – What's Love, 1993 – was over so we went our
own way. Two years later they wanted me back for the
Wildest Dreams tour of 1996. It was decided that I would
not go because Lejune wasn't going and I was in the middle of my master's degree, and you know, at some point I
realised I didn't want to be fifty and following Tina Turner
around. I wanted my own career. I did want to be at home.
I would never have met my husband.

Ann went on to found, with her then husband, one of the most
well-known rehabs in the world, Promises, nestled in the hills
overlooking Malibu. These days it's chock-full of celebrities, but
initially it was a modest affair designed to help those nearly
destroyed by addictions of every kind. Clients have included
Robert Downey Jr and Diana Ross.

In the eighties, when I was not working with Tina, I met
my first husband Richard Rogg and we started Promises – a
drug and alcohol rehab. We started that programme; it's
become very famous now. When I left to go on the road, he
continued with the company. When I came back we tried
to make the marriage work, but we split up and I sold my
half to him – and he's just sold it for a lot of money! That
helped launch my career as I specialise in substance abuse
and related issues. So I worked a lot with Promises and at the
rehabs in town [LA and environs]. I know everybody in the
business. I worked at UCLA at the Chemical Dependency
Certificate Program for eight years. I started a network-

ing group for women called the Women's Association for Addiction Treatment. I've done odds and ends and I've had a private practice for fifteen years.

After she started her practice, Ann frequently encountered people she had known on the road.

I didn't go around telling people I worked with Tina Turner. It helped because I've had a life beside being a therapist, and people in the entertainment world understand that I had a life and that I understand what it's like. I am a role model for people who want to be sober on the road because you don't have to drink and use.

With her experiences on the road behind her now, how does Ann feel about them?

Really good. I grew up with Tina. I feel like she was a mother. She could be like me sometimes because she was kind of playful and tough. Tough in a fun way. I have only good feelings for her. I wish her only the best. I think she's an amazing woman. I feel very grateful that I got to spend some time on Planet Earth with her and that energy.

Though clearly a positive influence on Ann, Tina Turner remains inscrutable.

She's a very, very private person and has a small group of people. She has a lot of ex-back-up dancers. I was thinking somebody should write a book or make a doc. There are at least twenty or maybe fifty people who have worked with Tina; some worked with her for a month, some for years. Lejune worked with her the longest. I broke the white-girl record after a year, that's what they told me. I'm very proud of that.

I think she has a very close life with the people who are very dear to her. I think she's doing good.

In spite of Ann's change of career, she can't stop dancing.

I dance at least four times a week. I do hip-hop classes. I dance my butt off. I just love it and people come up to me and they go, 'Oh my God. Oh my God, you are so great!' I look at them and say, 'I have a totally unfair advantage,' and they say, 'What's that?' and I say, 'I was a professional dancer.'

Thank God I have a place I can go. I probably could go to more classes but I have my little routine at the Sports Club LA. They've got some really good hip-hop teachers, Odell and Will. Odell Howard danced with Usher and all these guys. He's the real thing. So I'm lucky I get a chance to dance my butt off.

Ann recalls some scary moments from her dancing career, the kind of thing unlikely to happen on the therapist's couch.

I remember being onstage when Tina was in the red, not in the black, so we were doing these little gigs, two shows a night, and they were like doing aerobics and singing at the same time, twice a night. We were in Australia and I remember Kenny Moore [a fellow dancer] pointing to the floor, and I looked down and the floor had separated and there was this gaping hole with a guy with this hammer trying to hammer the floor together, you know, and we were dancing on this floor. Stuff like that. All kinds of crazy things . . .

And even the best dancers fall down unexpectedly. Of course, it's how you make it look and how you recover that make the difference.

Sure, we fell down all the time. Tina said she had never seen anybody fall like me because I was taught in dance that when you fall you 'act' like it's part of the dance and you get up dancing. She said, 'Girl, I saw you fall down on your butt and I saw that arm come up and you just kept moving,' so she took that from me. If you ever see her fall down and you see that arm come up, know that's from me! Falling is just inevitable when you're a dancer and you just get up and keep dancing.

Ann recalls the evening when Turner realised she had the support of her peers for her solo efforts. It was quite a night.

I remember the show that really changed her career, the show that put her back into the black. I think she had done 'Lets Stay Together' and we were at the Ritz in New York City. We had every famous person in the audience. David Bowie et al. And they were all just rooting for her. That was a real high point in her career and that was lots of fun.

Were there many after-show parties?

Tina very rarely hung out after a gig. When she did, it was in the early days when we all had to get on the bus to the next gig. So we were all together and she would just go to sleep. She wasn't much for going to the bar and trying to hook up and meet people or anything. We would all unwind – very often it was on the tour bus or at the hotel or whatever. Very often we've had some pretty wild times with the band and I've been the one dancing on the table, stone cold sober. Then I'd leave and I'd be getting up in the morning, ready to exercise, and they'd be in bed with the hangover. 'Bye, I'm going for a run!'

Ann showed me a clip from the internet. It shows Ann with her long hair, flying around Tina Turner onstage.* These days Ann wears her hair much shorter.

---

* youtube.com/watch?v=iqs8JNCx4dA.

I had hepatitis C and had to do interferon and ribavirin in order to get rid of it. I never had any symptoms of hepatitis C but I had a lot of the virus in my body and I did have liver damage; so I did the treatment and one month into the treatment I realised I was going to lose my hair. I lost almost all my hair and cut what remained to my shoulders, and I love it. So when I dance I don't flip all this hair but I can flip my shorter hair around and I love it. Besides, I looked like an old hippy with long hair. It was time for it to go.

8

I Was Moazzam Begg's Lawyer

One day there was this young woman who came in,
trembling like a leaf. Moazzam told me that he said, 'What's
wrong? Can I help? What's up?'
   Finally, she said, 'Well, is it true?'
   'Is what true?'
   'Is it true that you're Hannibal the Cannibal?'

Afghanistan had been largely left to rot after the American-
financed mujaheddin sent the Soviet invaders packing in 1989
with superior Western armaments, carefully disguised to look
as though they hadn't come from America. But the damage
had been done and the Red Army left behind a devastated
country.

In 2001 Birmingham-born Moazzam Begg was living in
Afghanistan, helping to establish a new school and improve
water facilities for locals, when he heard that, following the
Twin Towers attacks in September that year, American troops
were going to invade the country, overthrow the Taliban government and attempt to destroy Osama Bin Laden's Afghan
network of al-Qa'idah training camps, along with his fanatical
followers.

Wanting no part of the upheaval and hoping it might be
over fairly quickly, Moazzam left Kabul with his wife and family for Pakistan, where he stayed with friends. As Moazzam
writes in his book *Enemy Combatant*, he was dragged from his
friends' house by a squad of American and Pakistani troops
and interrogated at a local army base. From there he was sent

to Bagram military airbase in Afghanistan, then to the US-run detention centre at Guantánamo Bay in Cuba.

Unbeknownst to him, the Pakistani government, at the behest of the American administration and its military, had offered bounties of up to $5,000 to those living in the Afghan border areas for information about anyone connected with al-Qa'idah. In that region, $5,000 is a *lot* of money.

After being exposed to vigorous interrogation by the CIA (read 'torture') and kept in solitary confinement for the best part of two years in Guantánamo Bay's Camp Delta, Begg was contacted by US-based British civil-rights lawyer and dedicated Death Row specialist Clive Stafford Smith. They very quickly became friends, as Clive was not afraid to ridicule the US administration and expose the CIA's sometimes barbaric interrogation techniques. The events that followed were bizarre and terrifying in equal measure. Clive secured his client's release by writing a letter to Prime Minister Tony Blair, the bulk of which was redacted by the US State Department. Bizarrely, however, the letter's subject line – 'Re: Torture and abuse of British Citizens in Guantánamo Bay' – remained uncensored. Clive arranged for the letter to be published in a British national newspaper.

Since leaving Guantánamo, Begg has written a book and is engaged in an ongoing project to help fill the vacuum of ignorance and fear that followed the criminal horror of the attacks on New York by Bin Laden's suicide bombers, which Western governments have made little attempt to ameliorate.

Clive stressed at all times that neither he nor Begg has a personal axe to grind, just an unalloyed desire that those in government should appreciate the mistakes and misunderstandings that have led to these continuing breaches in 800-year-old jurisprudence, and to lift the veil of secrecy that both the American and British administrations are so fright-

ened of raising for fear of embarrassment. Terror seemed like
a good place to start.

*

Terror is a very unhelpful term, isn't it, really? It seems to
me we have this debate going on at the moment where
they have their T-word, which is 'terror', and we have ours,
which is 'torture', and you inject either word into the debate
and everyone becomes totally irrational. Take 'torture': if I
say, as [US defence secretary] Donald Rumsfeld did, that
I'm going to use my enhanced interrogation techniques
to break you, but it's not torture, who cares if it's torture?
I'm trying to break you. The whole thing's ridiculous. And
so the use of the word 'torture' actually justifies you doing
all sorts of insane other things, and the whole 'terrorism'
word is equally useless because it encourages people to
think that any act by people in those circumstances is 'terrorism', whereas, of course, if you talk to the Irish or to
any group of people who've wanted to overthrow the yoke
of some oppressor, whether you agree with them or not,
they certainly don't view it as anything other than necessary
warfare. I interviewed [renowned civil-rights lawyer] Alan
Dershowitz for something one time, and he was part of a
project, which was fascinating actually, where the question
is this: a bus is travelling down a steep road in San Francisco
or wherever and you're the driver. If you carry straight on,
you're going to plough into thirteen people and kill them
all. If you swerve off to the right, you're going to hit one
person and kill them. Which do you do?

You can't stop, so you've only got two choices. You've
either got to kill thirteen or one.

I'll kill one.

OK, second question, same scenario. Thirteen people ahead of you; you can turn off to the right and you can badly injure one person. Which do you do?

I'll badly injure one person.

Yeah. Now, third choice is that there are thirteen people ahead of you who you're going to kill, or you can turn off to the right and you'll torture one person. Which are you going to do?

It's the same thing, isn't it?

But you're torturing them.

When you torture someone, you injure them – the difference is you do it intentionally.

No, no, no. By swerving to the right you're going to torture that person. Which are you going to do?

Is it possible to torture someone unintentionally?

Look, you've got to answer. Don't fight the hypothetical.

OK.

You're either going to kill thirteen people or you're going to torture one person. Which do you do?

This is very—

The point of this whole debate, which you're obviously struggling with, is that . . .

. . . I would have to torture one person to avoid the death of thirteen.

You have a hard time with that don't you?
     By using the word 'torture', suddenly something shifts to

a different side of your brain. And it's ridiculous. It's just the injection of one word. You're not even killing that person, and yet you have problems with it.

It's a very interesting scientific study, and it illustrates how emotional and irrational we become in this debate.

Clive's background and upbringing could not be further from those he would go on to represent as a lawyer.

I grew up on a stud in Newmarket, Cheveley Park Stud. When I was about twelve, it was in the middle of the depression, my dad bankrupted it. So we went from being a bit nouveau riche to not being quite so.

We moved to Cambridge at that point. I was very fortunate and privileged. I went to private schools the whole time. I was studying Physics, Chemistry, Mathematics and Further Mathematics, just because, apparently, one does. I thought it was horrendously boring, and I was meant to go to Cambridge to study Natural Sciences. There's this whole road of your life that's mapped out into the dimmest distance, and I just didn't want to go down there. There was another reason. My older brother had gone to Cambridge and my mother, bless her, was admissions secretary at King's College. The idea of spending my dissolute university years at the same place as my mother, so she would know about all the wicked things I'd get up to, was just not a good plan.

As luck would have it – and this was totally unplanned, as almost everything in my life is – I was offered this place at the University of North Carolina at Chapel Hill on some incredibly generous programme. I had no idea where it was. I applied to a particular dormitory to live in because it said it had Connor Beach outside and I assumed that was the beach with the ocean. In fact, it was two hundred miles from the seaside. I hadn't even looked at a map before I went out there.

In America you didn't really have to apply for a course. I'd applied to do Natural Sciences at Cambridge, but at UNC you just went and drank too much weak beer, which I think was the main facet of it. So I did Political Science for the most part there.

I had this obsession with the death penalty before I went to America, but the programme I was on in UNC would have you do things in the summer. The first summer I went to work with the Los Angeles Sheriff's Department, and I will say that with cops like that you really have no need of criminals. It was quite a place.

I was in a real argument with some Los Angeles sheriff one evening over a drink and he was saying how we should execute all these people, and I was saying he was a lunatic. So he said, 'I know just the communists you ought to go work for.' He told me about this chap called Millard Farmer in Atlanta. The next year, rather than do what the scholarship programme made you do, I got them to pay for me to go and do what I wanted to do. So I went and worked with Millard down in Atlanta on the death penalty.

Millard was this fascinating guy, with an amazing Southern accent that I could barely understand, who had been brought up very wealthy and had rejected his family's Southern conservative roots and spent his entire fortune defending poor people facing the death penalty. I love Millard, and he used to offend everybody.

There was one time he was picking a jury and he was asking the jurors, as you're allowed to in America, 'Does anyone have any bias or prejudice against my client?' – his client not being white. One of the jurors sticks his hand up and says, 'Mr Farmer, I got a prejudice, but it ain't against your client, it's against you,' and started going on about what a commie pinko liberal Millard was. I thought that was fantastic.

At the time, my great aspiration was to become a journalist, but I found a way to sink even further in the public estimation because I wrote this rubbish book – it'll be viewed only by my grandchildren – about a guy on Death Row, which I thought was going to be the seminal piece that would change everyone's opinion. But by visiting Death Row every day for six months I met all these guys who didn't have lawyers, and it was astounding to me that the richest country in the world would not provide lawyers to people on Death Row.

So, having gone to visit this guy Jack Potts for the umpteenth time when he was facing execution, I figured I'd better get a law degree. I went to law school in New York at Columbia. I really only went to law school for one purpose, and that was to do death-penalty work back in the South, so I wasn't very interested in law school, to be honest.

I spent most of my time volunteering on death-penalty stuff, and running an incredibly bad newspaper, which was quite fun. The Americans didn't have a sense about April Fool's Day, so one year I ran the newspaper on that date. On 114th Street there was this cathedral that they were building, St John the Divine. They've been building it for over a hundred years and it's missing one of the towers. So I went inside and took a picture, slightly out of focus, of the model inside showing what it was meant to look like. The front page of the paper was 'Miracle on 114th Street', and it showed the completed-overnight cathedral.

Various people came up to me during the day saying, 'I went down to the cathedral and it's not been finished.'

[*Laughs*] Anyway, I think the main point of my law-school time was just being silly.

You learn absolutely nothing in law school. I honestly, seriously, couldn't have found my way to the court house coming out of law school. Those sorts of law schools don't prepare you for representing poor people; they prepare you to go on a one-line metro subway down to Wall Street. So I came out of Columbia Law School profoundly ignorant about everything.

I went straight back to Georgia. I worked with Steve Bright in the Southern Center for Human Rights. We represented indigent people, poor people, who couldn't afford lawyers, which includes everybody on Death Row. Capital punishment, as they say, is when men without the capital get the punishment. And so we were just taking any crisis that came along. In the early days, if you had an execution date you had no choice – we ended up representing you.

Back then in the early eighties I think all of us thought that people on Death Row were probably guilty. I've got to say that changed over the years, it honestly changed. I think the system has become more fallible as it's become more politicised. In the early days I would have said about five per cent of Death Row were innocent, which is a pretty bad rate – one in twenty wrong. But now it's much higher. It's probably more like thirty per cent; it's really quite shocking.

I tried my first death-penalty trial less than a year out of law school. I honestly had no idea what I was doing, and I remember the very nice, very effective prosecutor. I was representing John Pope. He was accused of shooting someone as part of an armed robbery in a drugstore, and that had clearly happened. But there were two people involved: there was the poor guy who got shot, and then there was another woman in the drugstore. John was a robber, that was his profession, and he'd never got involved in harming anyone before. But what happened was, this woman jumped him from behind, when he was robbing them, and whacked him over the head with a broom. And he, I think, was semi-conscious when the gun went off.

Typically for these cases, they gave us no funds, no money, no experts, no nothing. So we ended up having to get an Olympic boxer to come and testify for us, a guy called Marvin Johnson, who testified how during the Olympics he'd been knocked out but he carried on, when he was apparently unconscious, and won the fight. He was a great witness but I didn't know what I was doing. John got sentenced to death, and it was an enormous relief to me when we got it reversed later on appeal.

My first two cases weren't successful, and that was because I was totally inexperienced and shouldn't have been allowed to do it.

There are a lot of other cases. There were some interesting ones. I remember, for example, there was a slew of people called Jerome who were seriously mentally disabled. In fact, two were called Jerome Holloway, amazingly enough, and both of them had IQs under fifty. Now, you get forty-five points for taking the test, so a table has an IQ of forty-five in the US. Both of these guys called Jerome Holloway, one in Alabama and one in Georgia, had IQs of forty-nine. They were unbelievably mentally disabled.

People thought, 'Forty-nine, that's half of a hundred, he's just half as smart as the rest of us.' But of course, that's not how it works. Jerome Holloway in Georgia would say anything, and the only evidence they had against him was his confession. In order to illustrate his limitations I asked him, 'Jerome, did you assassinate President Lincoln?' He had no idea what the word assassinate meant, but he would listen to the tone of your voice and respond in the way he thought would please you, so he said, 'Yes.'

So I said, 'Well, did you assassinate President Kennedy?' He said, 'Yes.'

This was back when Reagan was president, and I said, 'Did you assassinate President Reagan?' and he said, 'Yes.' I said, 'No, he's only brain dead, he's not really dead.' That was before the poor guy got Alzheimer's and you could joke about him. The only thing that Jerome understood was that people would laugh at him. He had no idea why. It was just so sad.

We did an IQ test one time of everyone on Death Row in Mississippi, and thirty-two per cent – almost a third of them – came out as mentally disabled under that standard. That was one of the shocking aspects of the process; it's so easy to convict those people, because they'll say whatever you want them to say.

There were a number of British people who ended up on Death Row. I think the first person whose case I got involved in was Kenny Richey, the Scottish guy who faced the death penalty in Ohio. I did his appeal to the US Supreme Court way back, in like 1987 – maybe even earlier.

Kenny ultimately, twenty years later, was released. I think the evidence is very strong that not only did he not commit a crime, but no one did. The apartment where this little child died burned down very probably because the child was a bit of a pyromaniac and would light matches. But it was a great tragedy, and it became more of a tragedy when they sentenced Kenny to death.

He lived in the same apartment building. The prosecution's theory was that he was trying to burn his former girlfriend's flat down. The little child was in the upstairs apartment, and the former girlfriend was in the downstairs apartment. The prosecution's theory was that in order to set fire to the downstairs apartment, he set fire to the upstairs apartment – which doesn't make much sense. It was an incredibly weak case, but it illustrates what you see in so many capital cases: when the emotions run so high, as they obviously do in the death of some poor child, then all sorts of things go wrong. I can't tell you the number of cases I've had over the years where a child dies under tragic circumstances, where probably no one killed them and probably it was an accident. But because everyone gets so emotional about it, someone's got to pay.

Bryan Kolberg, a guy who was on Death Row in Mississippi, was accused of the death of a two-and-a-half-year-old child who had, in my opinion, fallen off a bed. Her head had fallen five feet and, if you do basic calculations, would have hit the floor at around about fourteen miles an hour. Of course that could cause a fatal head injury. I am absolutely certain, based on everything I've known about the case over the years – and I've been involved in it for two decades – that this poor child died by accident. And yet five American doctors came in and swore up and down that it's physically impossible for a child to fall five feet and die. They're just wrong. This is sort of Flat Earth Society nonsense, and we see so much of it in the context of these cases.

We got Bryan off Death Row and got him a new trial. I did the retrial, where I'm certain that he's innocent, and it's a source of absolute confusion to me that twelve jurors can come back and say beyond a reasonable doubt this individual is guilty. Indeed, some of them wanted to execute him, for something that I think wasn't a crime. It must be very humbling, as well as being confusing, to be the prosecution lawyer in those circumstances where you manage to get a guy convicted when you're certain he's innocent.

There were a number of other British people. Another well-known one was Kris Maharaj, who I'm still trying to help get out of prison in Florida.

The problem for Kris is that not enough people care about him. October 1986 he was arrested, and now, twenty-three years later, again I'm utterly certain that he's innocent. I think we know who did it – an assassin for the Medellín drug cartel out of Colombia – and we tracked him down. It's a long, long story, but the bottom line is Kris is now in his seventies, has spent twenty-three years in prison, much of that facing the death penalty, for a crime he didn't commit.

Why do these dreadful miscarriages of justice continue to occur?

There are reasons why the system is set up to fail, and it's true in Britain as well as in America, although it's more true in America. The reasons are quite complex, in a way, but I can state them generally.

First, if you're poor you're going to end up getting a terrible defence lawyer almost always in trial. Second, if you're innocent and you say, 'I didn't do it,' and you get a bit hostile to the police, they always respond to that by saying, 'This guy's lying.' Then you get a jury in who have been hand-picked, as they are in America; they have to say they believe in the death penalty in order to sit on the jury, so a large number of people who would perhaps give you the benefit of the doubt are out of there already. The process is so politicised, insofar as you have elected judges, elected prosecutors, and in Florida you have elected defence lawyers for goodness' sake. So the whole system is set up in ways that unfortunately encourage some mistakes.

But then when you're on appeal it gets even worse. The

reason they put Death Row miles away in the middle of nowhere is that you're out of sight, out of mind. You're not given a court-appointed lawyer at all for your appeals, which means you're not likely to prevail. And then you have these crazy, crazy rules where the Supreme Court has said, for example, that whether you're innocent or not isn't relevant, under the US Constitution, to whether you should get executed. Now how crazy is that?

The system is structured in a way to cover up the fact that the emperor wears no clothes, and it's what makes it so very, very difficult to get justice for some people.

Of course, that gets exponentially exacerbated when you get to Guantánamo Bay.

There are now many more that we're finding on Death Row round the world. Reprieve, the charity that I work with, we're now trying to help all British nationals facing the death penalty round the world. Not because British people have more rights than others; it's just that you have to limit what you do somehow, because there are so many people who need help. In this case we're able to get a lot of political support for them because, notwithstanding the failures of the British government in the past, they are getting better, at least at supporting people in capital cases. They're not so good on some of the other cases, but in death-penalty cases they're improving.

The whole issue of the death penalty was a politicisation of the problems. Look, in America you have some very, very serious social problems. So, for example, the crime rate is very high, there's a massive drug problem, you've got guns everywhere, and if you want to do something about that you have two choices.

One is to do something sensible, which is going to be quite difficult and politically difficult. You're going to have to start dealing with the causes of crime, which would involve getting rid of guns to begin with, and second it would involve a sensible approach to drugs and a sensible approach to poverty. The alternative is to do something fatuous, such as to say, 'We're going to kill a few people, and that somehow is going to solve the problem.'

Politicians, who have a rather limited shelf life, and certainly very little courage, always go for the second alternative, which is the fatuous one.

Clive recalled what went through his mind after the 9/11 attacks.

I remember very clearly when 9/11 happened, and it was horrific. I was in Lake Charles, Louisiana, doing a death-penalty case and trying to find some witnesses, and the place was a ghost town. I'd got up that morning, and I'd just seen the news and some little plane supposedly had accidentally flown into a building – at that point, that's what people thought. So I went out to find this witness, and I couldn't find anybody. By the time I got back to the place I was staying, we discovered what had really happened, and it was a total horror, a real crime of unparalleled proportions.

I remember the day after there were some very sensible questions being asked by some of the American media about 'Why are we so hated, why is this happening?' But that was very quickly swallowed up in this desire for revenge; something I underestimated, because when they created Guantánamo Bay, I thought it was horrific. It was so obviously wrong, and so obviously going to cause problems, that I immediately started calling around my friends so we could sue George Bush. I assumed everyone would want to do that, but actually America was terribly raw at the time, and I had misjudged it. It didn't stop me from wanting to sue him, but most of my death-penalty friends just didn't want to know, because this was the biggest shock to America since Pearl Harbor.

I had underestimated the fact that America had actually been victimised very rarely over the years from outside. You think about the war of 1812, you think about Pearl Harbor and you think about 9/11. Compare that to Europe and the horrors that Europe has gone through; it's a very, very different world.

Clive couldn't fail to notice the similarities between Death Row inmates and those incarcerated in Guantánamo Bay.

It was all exactly parallel. On Death Row you have hated people: black people, by and large. In Guantánamo Bay there were hated people: these guys with beards, Muslims. Death Row, you put them somewhere out of sight, out of mind, far away from lawyers and all the rest of it. Guantánamo, they put them in a different country where we weren't allowed to get close to them. And instead of saying, 'You don't have a right to an appointed lawyer,' in Guantánamo they said you didn't have a right to a lawyer at all. And so on and so forth. It was an exact, albeit exacerbated, parallel to Death Row.

Here we were, going around the world saying, 'We're here to teach you about democracy and the rule of law,' and the first thing we were doing was creating a prison without the rule of law. The hypocrisy of it was absolutely bound to get us into trouble, and that seemed obvious.

Politicians almost invariably make their rules with a hypothetical future crime in mind, so they're constantly looking for potential criminals who'll commit hypothetical crimes. What they're not doing is looking at what's actually causing crime.

For example: Guantánamo Bay. You can bang up seven hundred people, and those seven hundred people aren't going to commit a crime, so you're minimally safer from those seven hundred people. But at the same time you're actually inspiring, according to some CIA guy in 2004, seven *thousand* people to want to blow the US up. So your actions, far from making the world safer, are actually making it less safe.

You see this over and over again, with Belmarsh, with Guantánamo, with all these different things. Politicians take actions that may prevent an individual hypothetical crime, but they actually cause far more on the other side. To me, that's a betrayal of the people they're meant to represent. They're doing populist things that are just dangerous and foolish.

Clive was aware that Guantánamo, far from solving any problems, was going to make things much worse. In the rubble of universal tolerance, Clive found it hard to find any sympathy for those opposed to the idea of locking up potential terrorists.

When we first sued Guantánamo, which was February 2002, right after they'd opened it, we got British plaintiffs. I called around a bunch of my friends and I'd located Joe Margulies, another death-penalty lawyer I'd worked with, who was keen to do it. The only other person or group we found was Michael Ratner with the Center for Constitutional Rights, so we ended up being the three people to do it. We sued very early on, but it took two and a half years to get in. You had to have someone as a plaintiff, and we couldn't get the people in Guantánamo to do it because the Americans would shoot us on sight. The only way to get them represented was to find a family member, and the reason we had all British plaintiffs to begin with, and one Australian, was because they were open societies where the government told you who the prisoners were. We could track down their families and get their permission. So that's how Moazzam ended up being one of the early plaintiffs in the litigation.

It was this bizarre path that led Clive in November 2004 to the wire cell where Moazzam Begg had been held in isolation for over two years.

I went to see him. We'd got messages to him, because these prisoners had been kept in some total-isolation goldfish bowl for two and a half years at that point. Who were they to believe? What were they to believe? So many different deceptions had been played out on the prisoners – I didn't fully appreciate this at the time, but we had some inkling – they were going to think that these people showing up as lawyers were just a new form of interrogation. Indeed, the American military had used fake lawyers as part of their interrogation process to try to get people to talk.

At any rate, I had got an introduction from Moazzam's father saying who I was. They'd put my whole CV on there, all about how I only represented people facing the death penalty. Unbeknownst to me, poor old Moazzam was a bit panicked by this. He thought, 'Oh my goodness. That must mean they're going to execute me, the fact that they're giving me this lawyer who only does death-penalty cases.' So he was a little bit freaked out.

I went to see him in Camp Echo in Guantánamo Bay. You had to go through this bizarre palaver to get in – I mean, quite apart from having to sue them for two and a half years. They gave you a tour of the place before you could actually see your prisoner, and so they showed you around Camp Echo.

Guantánamo is an irony-free zone. They have the sign as you go in saying, 'Honour bound to defend freedom,' and here we are with all these people banged up with no freedoms. The military would salute each other and one would say, 'Honour bound, sir,' and the officer would salute back and say, 'To defend freedom, soldier.' I confess I laughed the first time I saw that; I thought it was a joke.

But then in Camp Echo they had a cell where they would take you, their model cell, and they'd show the comfort items. So you had your orange uniform, you had a game of checkers. I asked them, 'Who's he meant to play? He's in an isolation cell. Do you play with him?'

'Oh no, wouldn't do that.'

And then they had a toothbrush, a little mini-toothbrush. All these things, a very limited number of things, were meant to show what a wonderful place it was. I mean, it was a nightmare.

It was a PR process, but it was an incredibly misjudged one, as almost everything about Guantánamo was, because by showing you what they thought was the best of Guantánamo, they merely emphasised the very low minimum level at which they began. Then you'd start hearing the prisoner's version, and it could only go downwards from the level that the soldiers had purported to show.

I've got to say, I found the whole thing utterly bemusing when I first went there. But then I went in to see Moazzam, and you know, this whole stereotype: he was 'the worst of the worst of the worst'. I will confess that when Rumsfeld and Bush had said these were the worst of the worst people in the world, I assumed that my job was going to be pretty tough. I assumed that most of the prisoners were going to have been fighting in Afghanistan and we were going to have something quite difficult to explain. Whether it was any of

America's business that people were fighting in Afghanistan is a different question, but I assumed that that was going to be the battleground we would have in the courts.

You start meeting folk. I had a devil of a time finding anyone who had been fighting in Afghanistan. It became clear in Moazzam's case, as with so many others, that they'd all been turned over to the US for bounties. So someone had been offered three thousand pounds for any foreign Taliban; three thousand quid in that neck of the woods would be nearly a third of a million pounds to someone in Britain, say. And so I ask you rhetorically, 'Who are you willing to snitch on for a third of a million pounds?' And all you'd have to do is say, 'Oh, I saw that guy in Tora Bora.' Actually, probably a majority of people in Guantánamo Bay, far from being captured on the battlefield, were seized in Pakistan: they weren't even in Afghanistan. That was true of Moazzam Begg.

I met him, and instead of this stereotypical, terrifying terrorist, Moazzam is the nicest, politest man; he's like five foot three, wouldn't say boo to a goose. In Camp Echo you were totally isolated. The cell was cut down the middle with a sort of iron mesh, and the prisoner was kept over on the left-hand side. You had a bed and your comfort items and all that, and then on the right-hand side there was a shackle place where you'd be interrogated; so you never left that cell for the whole time you were there. Later they were allowed a little outside recreation in another little cage, but this was his entire world.

In the early days before they installed cameras, they had soldiers sitting in there. Moazzam told me this story about how he was in the cell and there was always, twenty-four hours a day, a soldier sitting on the other side of the wire grille, just staring at him, and forbidden from talking to him, allegedly. They were just meant to watch them. One day there was this young woman who came in, trembling like a leaf. Moazzam told me that he said, 'What's wrong? Can I help? What's up?'

Finally, she said, 'Well, is it true?'

'Is what true?'

'Is it true that you're Hannibal the Cannibal?'

Moazzam bursts out laughing, and it turns out all these poor soldiers, before they're sent into these cells, are filled up with this absurd propaganda about how evil the people were. This poor woman had been totally traumatised about Moazzam, and I think he spent the next three weeks giving her therapy. The wonderful thing about Moazzam is he's so unthreatening that he would end up making friends with many of the guards.

Clive noted that, while the attitude has now changed towards Guantánamo, sympathy for the inmates was once very hard to find.

Nowadays, people act as if the British media and British people were always against Guantánamo Bay. That's just not true. Up until June 2003 it was incredibly difficult to get anyone to show any sympathy for the prisoners there. It was a miscalculation on the part of the American military that helped us out. Of the first six people who were charged for the military commission process in Guantánamo, two were British and one was Australian. So you had Moazzam Begg and Feroz Abbasi from Britain, and David Hicks from Australia. For all the fact that in Britain everyone had gone along with the Americans to that point, charging two of our guys just didn't go down too well. Suddenly in Britain there was much more sympathy, or perhaps it was just a bit of anger; that was very, very helpful to us because finally people started paying attention. Up till that point I'd got a certain amount of hate mail and all the rest of that good stuff.

So Moazzam was the first, and I had this fascinating time with him. I was totally unprepared for what Guantánamo was like. It had never occurred to me that one day I'd be sitting across the table from some British guy talking about how Americans had tortured him. This was just absolutely off the charts of my comprehension.

I spent three days on that first visit with Moazzam just debriefing him about what had been done to him. It was very important actually not to talk to people there about what they were alleged to have done because then you just seemed like an interrogator, so my theory was to talk to them about what had been done to them, as opposed to what they were supposed to have done. So I spent three days talking to Moazzam about how he'd been abused.

He told me all about it; I took down a thirty-page memo about it all. Under the rules back then, every word that a prisoner said to you in Guantánamo was classified, and so you couldn't say anything to the outside world unless the American censors allowed you to. This was a very strange thing. I'd never had experience before (a) of talking to someone about being tortured in that way, (b) of not being able to say that to anybody, and then being told it was all classified.

So they had this very strange system where, in order for me to reveal to anybody that Moazzam had been tortured, and he had been, I had to get their permission. I had to go back to Washington – I wasn't allowed to keep my notes – and then when I got to Washington I had to type them up and submit them to the censors, and they would tell me what I could reveal. I typed up thirty pages of how he'd been abused, and how he'd witnessed two murders, two homicides in Bagram Air Force Base in Afghanistan, committed by US personnel.

Every single word was censored and was classified. I asked them, 'Why? How can this possibly be secret?'

And they say, 'Ah well, this would reveal our methods and means of interrogation.'

Then there were a couple of pages in there about what I viewed as Moazzam's mental-health issues, of what he'd suffered, and how he was continuing to suffer. And I say, 'How can that be classified?'

And they said, 'Oh well, that's his privacy interest, isn't it? We can't let that out.'

This was an Alice in Wonderland world. In fact, we used to call it Kafkaesque; we used to run out of all these terms to describe it because they would become so hackneyed – so much *more* hackneyed.

In the end, that was a huge battle we had to fight to get anything like that allowed out. I wrote a letter to Tony Blair saying, 'Dear Mr Blair,' and at the top I wrote, 'Re: torture and abuse of British nationals by your mates the Americans.' Then I detailed for a few pages what had been going on, and at the end I said, 'Anything that's been taken out of this letter has been censored by your friends, the United States, because they don't want you and the British people to know how we're torturing British nationals. Yours sincerely, Clive.'

And they censored it all; it was two pages long, and they left in the heading at the top and the last sentence at the bottom. We published that in the paper to make them look stupid. This was the only way that we could get out the fact that they were covering up their own crimes, and this was a battle that's still going on, it's still happening today.

Everything that goes on in Guantánamo they try to keep secret.

This friend of mine, Joe Margulies, who was one of the other lawyers who first started the litigation, put it best. He said, 'Our job is to open Guantánamo Bay up to public inspection. If we open it up, they'll close it down, because their only interest is in keeping a secret place.'

Moazzam's story was, I thought, remarkable when I first met him. I later discovered it was actually fairly common. He'd been in Pakistan. He'd left Afghanistan when the fighting occurred – he was there with his wife and children; he wanted nothing to do with it. He thought, as I think many of us would have thought back then, that this was all going to be over in a few weeks, and then he'd go back to Afghanistan and carry on the work he'd been doing there. Here we are many years later, and of course it's not all over.

He had two different things he was doing, both of which are very, very well established. One is he was trying to set up a school [that girls could attend]. Notwithstanding everyone's prejudices about fundamentalist Muslims, here was a person who wanted girls to get a good education, and if you knew Moazzam, you'd know that he was very sincere about that. He'd had some troubles with that, and his secondary project was trying to bring water to places that needed it, and so he had a system to try to dig wells in particularly poor parts of Afghanistan. Cynics who don't think that's true are just wrong; we've got it very well documented that that's what he was up to.

When you look at Afghanistan today and you see the arguments going on under the Karzai government about whether we should have laws that force women to do things that you and I would consider reprehensible, what you're seeing is a society that's actually very different to our own. I don't for one second say that I support those views; I think they're totally wrong, but the same was true back in 2001. I think that if you met Moazzam you'd recognise that he has very enlightened views on the vast majority of things. You can certainly be in a country and not agree with everything that the government does. I think any of us who live in Britain today would probably say that. When you start judging people by the government that happens to be running the country they're in, I think that's a pretty unfair way to go around judging folk.

Of course, some people are guilty of the most terrible crimes, but for that guilt to be established there must be utterly compelling and irrefutable evidence against them. Gaining access to the evidence possessed by the US State Department has been one of Clive's greatest frustrations.

They wouldn't tell us if there was any evidence. One of the great things about Guantánamo was they wouldn't tell us who was being held there. And they wouldn't tell Moazzam where he was being held. This was an immensely frustrating aspect of it for him and for everyone else.

Even though they said they were going to designate him for prosecution, they hadn't actually told him what they were going to prosecute him for. So in those early days I had no earthly idea what they were alleging against him. One thing I did know is that they were going around still saying that he was the worst of the worst, and now that he was going to be prosecuted he was the worst of the worst of the worst. But they wouldn't actually tell you why.

There was a time when I seriously considered bringing defamation litigation against the United States for what they were doing, because they were basically just slandering him, but they wouldn't tell us why and they wouldn't let us have an opportunity to defend him.

What I don't understand is how anyone can look at this process and view it differently than the way we used to criticise the Soviet Union. We would say, 'Oh my goodness, those Soviets, they lock people up without trials, they do these awful things.' The Bush administration, and let's face it, the Blair government, would dress it up in fancy language, like in Belmarsh, for example, and say, 'Well, we've got to do it.' But when you look at it in the cold light of day, Moazzam Begg was being held without charge, without trial, just being banged up ad infinitum. The reason I've never used the word 'detainee', which seems to have become in vogue, is that that was a term adopted by the military to sound nicer, because if we're just 'detaining' you, it's like, 'I'll detain you for tea.' But if you 'imprison' someone, and you're a 'prisoner', then you're not 'imprisoned for tea'. That was the reason they chose that word, to be a kinder, gentler form of rubbish.

I found it terribly hard, having met the human being Moazzam Begg, to believe that he was anything like what they were saying, and he had a very credible story that checked out. Mind you, it was all very novel to me. I hadn't yet figured out how this was working. He told me how he was snatched up in Pakistan, and even Moazzam at the time didn't quite know how that had happened. It took us until later to find out this whole bounty process. Now, the US admitted that they were doing these bounties, and actually President Musharraf rather boasted in his tedious autobiography about how much money they'd made getting bounties from the Americans.

So the first step was an informant, as you have in many capital cases, pointing the finger at Moazzam, saying he was a wicked person. The second step was that the Americans would interrogate him, and Moazzam, because he was from the West, knew his rights and said, 'I've got nothing to say to you people.' That would immediately make them think that he was guilty, as the police do with a prisoner on Death Row. The difference here, of course, is that the police were allowed legitimately to start applying 'enhanced interrogation techniques'. They start torturing him. Moazzam told me about it, and I never thought that one day I would be researching what the Spanish Inquisition used to call these different techniques.

Strappado was the favourite one, where they would hang you by your wrists. It sounds relatively benign until you realise that it slowly dislocates your shoulders in an incredibly painful way. I sort of did it to myself playing cricket yesterday, so in a very light format I know what it's like.

Moazzam told me about all of this and he also described to me what was the worst, and that was surprising too. I hadn't really thought about it this way. He said second-degree torture was way worse than the direct thing, because if I came up to you and really abused you, it would be horrible but you'd know it was going to finish; and it was pain, pain, pain. But the anticipation of pain was worse.

Or, in his case, he said that the single worst thing was when they told him that they had his wife in custody, which was a lie. In Bagram there was a woman in the next room from him who was screaming in terrible pain, and they said that was his wife. He said that was far worse than anything they did to him, to think that they were torturing her until he would say what they wanted to hear.

The 'Guantánamo Four' – Feroz Abbasi, Moazzam Begg, Richard Belmar and Martin Mubanga – were all British citizens

held in US custody at Guantánamo Bay, accused of being ille-
gal non-combatants. The US authorities claimed that Belmar
was found at an al-Qa'idah safe house in Pakistan. Abbasi
was detained in the north of Afghanistan at Kunduz. The case
against the fourth man, Martin Mubanga, was complicated by
the fact that he had been the subject of an extraordinary rendition from Zambia to Guantánamo Bay and thus not captured
in the theatre of operations.

In November 2002, during an action brought by relatives of
Abbasi, the British Court of Appeal considered his detention
in Cuba to be 'legally objectionable'. However, the British government declined to intervene on his behalf.

All four men were returned to the UK in January 2005 and
questioned by police before being released without charge.

I've never seen any formal allegations against Moazzam, so
it's very hard to respond to anything against him. What I
have heard is some of my friends in the media who have
been briefed by the American intelligence agencies and military against Moazzam. When he was released to Britain,
far from saying, 'Oh look, we're sorry, we shouldn't have
banged you up this way in the first place,' they released
something to, I think, the *Telegraph* and the *Sun*, basically
saying really unpleasant things about the four people who
were released together. They didn't actually say who was
who, they said 'prisoner 1, 2, 3 and 4', but it was pretty
obvious who each person was.

Since then, they've continued to make statements to
different journalists about how Moazzam is some senior
al-Qa'idah member. It is absolute nonsense, and it is defam-
atory. I've written to the American government before now
saying if they carry on doing this we're just going to sue
them. Actually, I think Moazzam would have loved, and

I would like, a day in court where you could air all these allegations and make the other side put up or shut up. I have no doubt that what he says is true, but as we've always said, and Moazzam's said, if anyone wants to say something different, do what we've done for the last eight hundred years: charge him and give him a fair trial.

Clive suspects that many intelligence services manipulate internet resources as a means of spreading propaganda.

One of the fascinating things about Wikipedia and some of the other internet sites has been the misinformation or disinformation process that's been used by the American intelligence agencies to actually change them. We've caught them at it, changing the map of Guantánamo Bay, for example, and they go through changing a bunch of articles about different prisoners. This is pretty scandalous, and it is the very worst of the process, isn't it? Instead of giving you a fair trial, the government, with all its power, goes around altering the internet to basically defame you.

Moazzam has been taken down the road familiar to those acquainted with the experiences of Terry Anderson and Terry Waite, who were imprisoned against their will in Lebanon in the eighties.

I think Moazzam was always Moazzam. He was always a dignified, educated, decent person. I do think that, as with so many prisoners from Guantánamo, he gained, in a bizarre way, something from that experience. He gained a nightmare as well, I should emphasise that, but on the other hand this really gave him a perspective on the world. I think it's helped him in the sense of giving him a mission, which is a mission of reconciliation. I'm so pleased about so many of the people I've represented; that their response to the nightmare of Guantánamo isn't to be angry and want to blow America up, but instead to want to deal with the problem and to try to reconcile people instead of doing what George Bush did. That's very, very pleasing.

One of the things I wanted to do was try to help get Moazzam a grant, which he's got, from the Joseph Rowntree Charitable Trust, who are great; they're folk up in York, and they're very committed to religious reconciliation. They've funded him to do what he does best, which is to go round giving talks about how we shouldn't all hate each other.

Was Moazzam exposed to extremists before going to Afghanistan?

I've never really talked to Moazzam about that. From my own perspective, I've spent so much time in the Deep South of the United States, where we would deal with fundamentalist Christians who had some pretty strange views about women, about the rights of women, about marriage, about family, about the death penalty, about all these different things, that I just don't have conversations with people where I start interrogating them about their religious beliefs.

I think it's an element of our society, of our political society, that we're teaching people to hate folk for this. I may not agree with some religious views of some or many people, but that doesn't give me the right to go round quizzing them on it. I just don't see that as my role in life.

There are many reasons why people follow a particular religious faith, and I'm not going to generalise on that and tar everyone with the same brush. I deal with individual human beings; I don't deal with these swathes of stereotypes that the government deals in. In terms of the individual human being, Moazzam Begg, I've always found him to be

(a) incredibly dignified, (b) a very nice, decent person, and (c) someone who really does understand the country he lives in. And he understands something that it took me a while to learn in America, which is that if you're going to be heard by people, you've got to speak the language they speak, even if you have views that are quite different from theirs. Mine were very different from a lot of jurors in the Deep South, but if I could speak their language, then I could get them to see the world through my eyes. After the two catastrophes of my first two trials, I'm glad to say no jury ever came back with the death sentence again, because I'd learned not to be quite so stupid, and I'd learned to speak the language that they would hear.

In that sense, Moazzam speaks very well, and he goes around Britain doing so. I remember this great story. He was giving a talk in one place, a big crowd and a bunch of posh people, and in one of the front rows was one of these Lord Justices from the British courts. The guy came up to Moazzam afterwards and said, 'I didn't realise there were people like you in Guantánamo Bay.'

I think that's wonderful. Everyone has the stereotype about what people were like in Guantánamo, and here's Moazzam and he just doesn't fit any of them. I used to always take people to Death Row who'd tell me they were in favour of the death penalty, and never in a quarter-century of doing that have we ever come out without them changing their mind. And it's just because you suddenly meet the real person as opposed to the stereotype. You've got sixty million British people; you can't take them all onto Death Row to meet individual people, so it's hard to show them the individual reality.

There's a big difference, I think, in the position that Moazzam found himself in compared to, for example, [IRA hunger striker] Bobby Sands, in that Moazzam was utterly, utterly cut off from everything. When I went to see him, I was basically the first human being from outside the prison setting he'd met for two or three years. In Northern Ireland people were allowed visitors; they were heavily publicised. That's how the Bobby Sands hunger strike did what it did. In Guantánamo Bay, everything possible was done to keep it secret.

I never had the sense with Moazzam that he was into 'martyrdom' of any sort, and certainly not into starving himself to death. He was actually in a fairly unique position in Guantánamo: he was kept isolated from almost all the other prisoners in these isolation cells in Camp Echo, which was very difficult for him. I think one reason why he made so many friends with the guards is they were the only people he *could* make friends with, and he was good at making friends. It's a tribute to him that, after he left, some of these guards, who began with such stereotypes about him, maintained a friendship with him.

There was one guard who I quite liked, but he took his hat off and in the rim of his hat it said 'Al-Qaeda are pussies'. [*Laughs*] And you just thought, 'What inspired him to write that inside the rim of his military hat?' But he was a pretty nice guy, and when he got talking, he would listen, so he wasn't close-minded.

But Guantánamo wasn't all being stared at twenty-four hours a day and playing checkers with yourself.

We laughed about a lot, actually. I do view it as one of my roles in visiting prisoners, to sort of cheer them up, and I don't want to go in there and have some serious conversation for three days. It was pretty tough, the serious stuff we did talk about, but we laughed about a whole bunch of things.

I would tell him all sorts of stories about the American judicial system. We'd have a good laugh about what morons the Bush administration were, because you had to. It was part also of my own sense of trying to make friends with people and get their trust: you had to speak fairly frankly about our political leaders. I'm glad that since Moazzam's got out he's said that he found it refreshing that someone came in and said various things about George Bush that I can't repeat because I think they'll get censored out, but they're things that I believe are totally true. I'm not a big fan of George Bush, any more than I am of Tony Blair.

Some lawyers who would go into Guantánamo Bay later on, who took the whole thing far too seriously in my opinion, would give their clients a long lecture about how 'this is all confidential, this is part of the attorney–client privilege, let me tell you about the attorney–client privilege'. To the prisoners, this just made them total idiots. Of course, people were listening in. In fact, when you were in the cells, if you wanted to leave, if the client wanted to go to the toilet or whatever, you would press the button and say, 'Can my client go to the bathroom?' Then they would talk, and they would listen to you without any button being pressed, so they could clearly listen to everything you did. And if you want to lose your client's trust in an instant, you'd say, 'This stuff is all confidential.'

I would tell Moazzam that I had a thing going with my wife where we're convinced that they look at my email. I've been told by American military people they do. I'm very sorry for them; I think they must get terribly bored. Emily and I would have this thing where we would send emails to each other that would be to the CIA, saying 'Look, we're really sorry we've been so tedious. We're going to have a conversation now about our dog,' and we'd assume that some poor CIA person would have to read that. I would tell things like that to Moazzam just to make it perfectly clear that I knew we were being listened in on. But I've got no problem; the only way to get the CIA to listen to you is to have a conversation.

Common sense, so called because not many people have it, appears to have descended like a clear fog – for now. The Barack Obama administration has pledged to close Guantánamo Bay, which may actually make things worse for the unwanted guests at America's sunniest offshore 'enemy combatant' prison.

I think that the people in the White House would like to establish the American system as it should be, but they live in an ivory tower that's way divorced from the real world. Emily has this lovely Australian saying, which is that politicians, judges and folk like that need to have the 'long brown envelope of home truths' delivered to them every now and then. I love that phrase, and it's true that people who are high up are so divorced from the real world they have no idea about what's really going on.

It's a total myth to think that there's suddenly been a shift in attitudes in Guantánamo. In fact, in some ways things get worse, because I think the people on the ground have lost the notion that they have the moral high ground; they're very depressed, and staff morale is very low in Guantánamo because of what happened. They no longer have a president who's saying, 'Justice is on your side.' They have a president saying 'This is a nightmare.' So of course they feel bad. This is something my granny told me: if you know that you're mistreating another person, it's your natural human nature to hate them for it. You, the perpetrator of the wrong, hate the victim. That's just normal, and it's the reason why I always tell the prisoners in Guantánamo, 'We've got to be twice as nice to them now because they're going to hate us regardless.'

It's always been true that there are one or two prisoners in Guantánamo Bay who end up as the beacons for everybody. In Moazzam's case, it was true not only of him, but also of his father. His father is this wonderful, dignified gentleman, formerly in banking, had heart problems, who would wear his heart on his sleeve, and who simply would not stop. Even when his doctor told him he shouldn't go on, he would carry on being the advocate for Moazzam, and we desperately needed that.

It was one thing me trying to speak for him, but that's not nearly as effective as a human being who's really emotionally attached. It was very clear to us that the court of public opinion was going to be much more important than the court of law in this process. Indeed, if you look at the first five hundred prisoners released from Guantánamo Bay, zero were released through a court order and five hundred were released through public pressure. Moazzam was a great example of that: his father would come around to the events we would organise and be the spokesperson, and I think people would see his dad and would say, 'How could the son of that man be the nutcase that Donald Rumsfeld and George Bush say he is?' That was the best way to humanise Moazzam until he could do it for himself.

Did the Guantánamo prisoners really have no idea where in the world they were being held?

Moazzam had a pretty good idea he was in Cuba. Some prisoners didn't believe it even when I'd tell them; they thought they were in North Africa. You had obviously a similar climate, and you knew what the climate was, but you had no idea otherwise. It made no sense to a lot of Arab people that the Americans would have a base in Cuba, because one thing you knew about America and Cuba is they hated each other.

I'd dealt with Guantánamo beforehand because of the way they'd treated the Haitian refugees, but not many people knew that.* Indeed, Guantánamo's name has been tarnished for evermore. Though I should say there was one really nice African American escort who would take us around, whose great ambition was to create a holiday vacation spot in the Caribbean. He said, 'Look, it's got great name recognition, all publicity is good publicity, it's got a good airport, it's got hotels with incredibly solid, secure rooms – because they're cells – and it's got everything going for it.' So that's his ambition one of these days.

After years of incarceration one would expect Moazzam to be just a little hacked off. Not so.

Moazzam is far more forgiving of the Bush administration, or certainly of the American people: he holds nothing against the American people, though he does think the Bush administration were profoundly misguided. And he is very positive about British society. I think he's not quite so positive about some of the attitudes of British politicians, but he's someone who really lives what he believes, which is reconciliation. He's done more good certainly than Tony Blair in terms of trying to reconcile people from two different faiths. I'm glad to see Tony Blair's setting up his Faith Foundation. He's got quite a lot to make up for over the last few years.

---

* Thirty-five thousand Haitians fled their homeland after a violent coup in 1991 and were put in a string of holding camps named after the phonetic alphabet, Guantamo's Camp X-ray being one of them.

I think almost anyone who's met Moazzam, or heard him speak, is immensely impressed with him. The British Establishment is still a bit afraid of him. I have told them, 'Look, if you people want to do anything sensible, you need to embrace him.' This is the sort of person who can help reconciliation, much more than the folk that the government tends to go towards, who are the people who are profoundly on their side, by which I mean people who will say horribly negative things about everyone else.

You're not going to get Moazzam to tar people with the brush of extremism. He's not going to say of anybody, except perhaps Bin Laden, that these people are all insane. He's met some of these folk who are deemed to be such extremists and he knows them as human beings, as I know them. In consequence, he knows that they're not the monochromatic people that the government would have you believe. Not everyone who was in Guantánamo was a saint or whatever, but none of them are the uniformly wicked, evil people that they're made out to be. All of them have a story, and it's a story that it's very important for us to understand, because if we don't understand it, we're just going to exacerbate the problem.

Clive's greatest fear is not that the lessons won't be learned but that the administrations implicated in these actions aren't prepared to admit the truth and move on.

One of the most dangerous things, and Moazzam would certainly say this, even worse than the torture – and that is horrific, but I think we're going to win the torture battle – is the secrecy battle. What we've seen over the last eight years or more has been an exponential rise in the US and UK governments' effort to maintain things as secret. If there's one lesson you inevitably learn from history, it's that if you don't know what history is, you're not going to learn from it. So we're doomed to repeat these problems if we don't reveal how it was that we came to this catastrophic experiment with torture and secret prisons. We've got to know that. And you see governments trying to cover that up, whether they be American or British, all the time, and that's terribly wrong.

It's conflating national security with national embarrassment. And it's saying that if a government fears it's going to be embarrassed, it can say, 'This is secret.' An extreme example of that is the British government's effort to edit out everything embarrassing about their expenses. If it weren't for the fact that someone leaked it to the *Telegraph*, we wouldn't know an awful lot about ponds and duck houses and all the rest of it. Now, how can that possibly be a matter of national security or a matter of secrecy? It's not; it's a matter of embarrassment.

Moazzam Begg's *Enemy Combatant* is his account of his shocking experience at the hands of the US military.

I think it's very important that Moazzam wrote his book, and I encouraged him to do it for two reasons. One was for his own personal catharsis, but second, if you're going to overcome the anathema of secrecy, then the only way to do it is to put the truth out there. I was involved somewhat in his writing his book. My only real criticism is he understates a lot of what was done to him. In a way, that's good. I think he did it for the best reasons: he didn't want to make his own abuse the focus of the story, as that doesn't contribute to reconciliation. But I think that's a very positive aspect of the book. Everyone should read it.

When you think about Britain and America, and America being starved for information, one way that they're starved for information is that no one like Moazzam can go to America. If Cat Stevens is banned from entering because he wrote too many songs called 'Peace Train', Moazzam Begg and folk like that simply can't go and do a speaker's tour of America, which is a great, great shame, because the Americans actually are the ones who most need to hear it. The second best thing is for his book to be published there, so I'm very pleased he did that.

It's not hard to see why administrations and governments use extant threats to their own ends. Y2K? Swine flu? Global warming? The trouble is someone, somewhere can join up the emails now. Remember, al-Qa'idah can never take away your human rights. Only politicians can do that.

I know that it went all the way to the White House: there's no question about that now when you see all of these different documents that have come out. And of course that makes logical sense. If you take the case of Moazzam being rendered, or more one of the individual cases like Binyam Mohamed being rendered to Morocco for torture, there's no way some little CIA person's going to do that all on their own.* They're going to get cover, and they're going to get it probably from the National Security Council, the NSC. There's a lot of information that tends to show that.

---

* Mohamed, an Ethiopian national, arrived in Britain in 1994 seeking political asylum. His application was rejected but he was given exceptional leave to remain in the UK for four years. According to the US authorities, he was fighting on the front line against anti-Taliban Northern Alliance forces. He was arrested in 2002 and imprisoned in Morocco for eighteen months, then transferred to Guantánamo via Afghanistan. In 2009 the charges against him were dropped and he was returned to the UK. In February 2010 the UK Court of Appeal ruled that the British government must disclose US-supplied evidence concerning the case, stating that Mohamed had been subjected to 'cruel, inhuman and degrading treatment by the United States authorities'.

The reason I think it's desperately important for us to reveal that is not because I want to persecute those people; I don't, and I know Moazzam doesn't. It's that we've got to explore how they reached the decisions to do this, because if we don't explore that then we can't prevent it from happening in the future. Personally, I'm hugely in favour of truth and reconciliation commissions, and I think Moazzam is too, but you can't have reconciliation without truth. You can't say to the world, 'Well, we made a terrible mistake here, we're not going to tell you what it is, but we want you to forgive us.' That just doesn't work.

'Sorry' is a fascinatingly difficult word for people to pronounce and totally easy to say. I have the advantage of having a British passport and an American passport, and as I go around the Middle East trying to meet with families of prisoners and so forth, I always begin by saying, 'Look, I apologise on behalf of both Britain and America.' And while some may think I don't have a right to say that – and I do say, 'Look, obviously I'm speaking for me, not for the government' – it immediately opens every door, to say 'I'm sorry'.

You see so many politicians making mistakes. We've sued them so many times in recent weeks and months over British complicity in torture and so forth. If they would just put their hands up and say, 'We're sorry,' that would be great, but they won't.

Surely that's not completely true. Saying sorry is now becoming part of the glib armoury of the political establishment. Even so, words won't restore trust or right legal wrongs, will they?

I think there's a more specific hypocrisy involved in these apologies. One of the best examples would be the rendition from Iraq case that we brought against the British government, where the British admitted in early 2009 that with the Americans they had rendered two people from Iraq to Bagram Air Force Base in Afghanistan, where five or six years on they were still being held without the least due process.

They admitted they did that; they said, 'We're sorry, we shouldn't have done it.' So I immediately wrote to the Ministry of Defence, saying, 'What are the names of these two people, and will you please help us reunite them with their legal rights?' They wouldn't do it. They wrote back saying, 'We won't tell you their names because that would violate their privacy rights under the Data Protection Act.'

Really, the parallel is this, to me: let's say that a member of the Mafia comes to a press conference and says, 'Look, I want to apologise for the fact that I kidnapped a couple of people.'

And you say, 'Well, that's really good. Now, who are the victims of this kidnapping?'

'Oh, I'm not going to tell you that.'

'And where are they now? Are you going to help us get them out?'

'Oh no, we're not going to let them go.'

The Metropolitan Police would arrest the guy at that point as an ongoing member of a kidnapping conspiracy. And the idea that the government can pretend that they've actually given a meaningful apology when the victims are still banged up in Bagram is just absurd.

Setting aside the colossal failures of humanity, how do individual victims come to terms with what has happened to them?

Moazzam will never get closure. You don't go through the abuse and torture he went through and ever get closure. I think he's dealt with it far better than most people, but one thing that I worry about is that people forget what he's been through, and that he constantly has to relive it in the sense that when you go around and talk about it, you *are* reliving it, and I'm not sure that's totally healthy for him. I think it's very beneficial for society, but not always for him.

I think that the most important thing for Moazzam is that he continues to have a fulfilling professional life, helping with reconciliation, while at the same time doing what he loves to do as a parent. One of the most terribly difficult things for him in Guantánamo was he'd had a child born who he'd never met. I've got a little boy myself and the idea of missing the first three years of his life would be a terrible tragedy.

For Clive, his friendship with Moazzam Begg has been an enlightening experience.

In many ways my experience with Moazzam has been similar to those with people I've represented on Death Row, insofar as when we've been lucky enough to get them out of prison, we've become friends. I do consider Moazzam a friend, and I have the greatest respect for him, I really do.

I've learned so much over this. I knew nothing about Islam; I knew nothing about any of those issues before I got involved in Guantánamo Bay. Moazzam is a very reasonable recounter of issues involved in Islam; it's been a very educational experience for me. It's reconfirmed in many ways my own perspective on the world, which is that broad-based sweeping generalisations criticising a group of people are almost inevitably wrong. It's not to say that we don't have different views on the world, but most of those can be reconciled, and certainly the way to resolve them is not by locking people up without trial.

As we tiptoed down the stairs so as not to wake up his sleeping son, I realised I was in the company of a unique person.
The boy had fallen asleep listening to Clive and me discussing
the importance of telling the truth, being open and replacing
hatred with understanding. We were all asleep at the wheel of
an oil tanker, owned in our name by Bush, Bin Laden and Blair.

9
I Was Sam Peckinpah's Girl Friday

I often think, what would have happened if she'd come
through with a frying pan and cold-cocked him?
    Ali MacGraw

Sam Peckinpah was one of the last great Hollywood directors
to have cut his teeth making TV westerns. The western, always
seen first as a fail-safe revisionist record of American coloni-
sation, was under cultural assault in the sixties. With bloody
and obscene images of maimed young men on the television
news every night during the Vietnam War, the genre became
cynical, reactive and comical – from Sergio Leone's spaghetti
westerns to the lamentable musical *Paint Your Wagon*. Only Sam
Peckinpah, steeped in and descended from the same western
pioneers he portrayed in his films, appeared to understand
what was needed. He rode to the rescue in 1969 with *The
Wild Bunch*, redefining the violence of the American west by
openly violating the American dream and its jaded, desperate
romantics.

    Katy Haber was in her twenties when she became an assist-
ant to the legendary Hollywood director. She very quickly
became much more than that, but increasingly over time much
less of a human being. You might say it's not so much what Katy
did as what Katy was.

*

My job description was 'associate producer', but I was cred-
ited under many different titles. Sometimes I got no credit

at all. I was at Sam's side twenty-four hours a day, helped plan and schedule the shooting, worked on the call sheet with the second-unit director . . . Sam never went anywhere on the set without me.

Film critic Mark Kermode is a friend of Katy.

She enabled him to get the films made. She was Peck's other half. If she hadn't been there the films wouldn't have been made. She protected him and was the one person who understood him through all the mad periods.

Actress Ali MacGraw, the Oscar-nominated star of Peckinpah's *The Getaway* and wife of the late Steve McQueen, is also a close friend.

Katy was very much his Girl Friday and then some. She had to second and third guess his every wish, and be at the mercy of his rage fits – which he did from some complicated place inside of his tortured head, sometimes for theatrical effect. It could be incredibly cruel and humiliating, and he preferred to do it in public. It was difficult to watch, to put it mildly.

Mark Kermode explains the significance of Peckinpah's films.

We think of him [Peckinpah] as the great recorder of violence. This comes mainly from *The Wild Bunch*. It's an analysis of violence and it's about the nature of conflict. There is a debate about whether the balletic violence in *The Wild Bunch* revelled in it or turned it into a visceral experience. The film made him the great poet of screen violence.

Paradoxically, Katy's career, so steeped in the violence of the Wild West, began in genteel SW19. It's June 1970 at the All England Lawn Tennis and Croquet Club. The Wimbledon

Championships are under way. The covers are off, the sun is out and Katy Haber is a full-on Wimbledon groupie. As she follows the bouncing ball with the other tenniserati, Katy gets a message that will change her life . . .

I was asked to call James Swann, associate producer on *Straw Dogs*. He said, 'Sam Peckinpah needs an assistant!' I'd never heard of Sam Peckinpah, but rang anyway. Sam said he had offices at Universal Studios. 'Can you be here in twenty minutes?' I said, 'I'm on the other side of London. It would take me about three-quarters of an hour to get there.' He said, 'Forget it, then.'

I didn't give it a second thought and continued watching Ralston playing Newcombe.

A week or so later I got another call from Swann saying Peckinpah was still looking for someone. 'He's had three people working for him since you called him.' It didn't work out because they wanted lunch breaks, hairdresser trips, etc. It wasn't quite what he had in mind.

When Katy rang him again, Peckinpah made the first of many demands.

'Can you be at Universal this afternoon?' he said.

I went and there was a grumpy guy behind a desk. The grumpy guy was Peckinpah. I said, 'My name's Katy Haber. I hear you want me to give you a second chance.'

He said, 'Can you type?'

He handed me a script – *The Siege of Trencher's Farm* by David Zelag Goodman.

Sam said, 'Help me with these rewrites.' Within a week we'd finished the screenplay and I was working for him.

The critical success of *The Wild Bunch* – due in no small part to its graphic, almost operatic violence – marked out the signature style of Sam Peckinpah: impotent rage, brutish male chauvinism and brutal casual violence are the hallmarks of this classic Peckinpah film. Peckinpah decided to explore further the competing themes of violence – latent, graphic and sexual, to name but three – in a movie that was to become his most complex and conflicted film: *Straw Dogs* (1971). Mark Kermode helps to unravel this compelling, cold and hostile film.

Straw Dogs is almost the defining work of Peckinpah. It's the film that best encapsulates the raging torment inside him. Pauline Kael [revered New York film critic] said that *Straw Dogs* showed a fascist mentality. It's a deeply troubling film. Sam's attitude towards men and women is deeply troubling.

Katy was compelled by the auteur director to help him write a now notorious scene from the film.

The first thing I wrote with Sam was the rape scene in *Straw Dogs*.

The scene is probably the most talked-about rape scene in any film ever made. It looks rather tame alongside the grindhouse meisterwerks of today's torture-porn splatter-film production line (*Hostel*, *Saw*, *The Collector* or the superior Lars von Trier film *Antichrist*, for example), but back then Susan George caused a storm with her performance. Yet Peckinpah wanted her to go even further than she was prepared to.

Mark Kermode explains how the conflict was resolved on the set.

The interesting thing about the rape scene – it's the memorable thing, and the heart of the film. Susan George fought with Peckinpah about how it should be shot. She recalls that Peck wanted it to be more graphic. Susan suggested expression through her face rather than graphically. After many serious, shoot-stopping fights, Susan agreed with Sam that she would shoot the scene her way – and if it worked, OK. She filmed it her way and Sam watched the rushes and went with it. The heroine is displayed as a profoundly duplicitous character. The film is the work of someone who is deeply suspicious of women.

I asked Katy whether the experience of writing such a disturbing scene together affected their emotional relationship.

If you want to be cerebral about it, yes; but the emotional contact was far more about his charisma. There's something about Sam that people need to understand. Throughout my career with him, I saw him seduce women just with his persona. There was something about him that was very seductive. Men, too.

Men really loved him. His crew loved him. His actors became him. William Holden was Sam in *The Wild Bunch*. Warren Oates was Sam in *Bring Me the Head of Alfredo Garcia*. And Jason Robards was definitely Sam in *The Ballad of Cable Hogue*.

If you asked someone what they thought of Sam Peckinpah, they never said, 'Oh, he's OK.' It was either, 'He's the greatest person I've ever met,' or, 'What an arsehole, what a pig, what a violent incorrigible human being.'

He's a very powerful person to be emotionally involved with, and very disloyal in some ways. I can tell you: I wasn't the only woman in his life in the eight years I spent with him – far from it. He was a very seductive person.

When did you become lovers?

The second night, I think.

Ali MacGraw believes that Sam Peckinpah's background may explain his unpredictable talent as a film-maker.

He was an aristocrat – part of the aristocracy of the Old West. He was educated and cultured. He had a beautiful heart, but whatever happened to him as a young man put a rather cruel streak in him. I understood totally the attraction – this was the story of 'when he was good . . .' When he was in his full charm he was irresistible.

Mark Kermode sheds further light.

Directors are not the same as ordinary people. A movie set is like a ship on the brink of mutiny. Once it sets sail your job is to take it across the ocean. You can't stop because there's so much money involved. There must be a firm hand on the tiller. You have to be reasonably socially inept. You have to be a megalomaniac in order to get your vision on-screen.

Katy worked with Peckinpah during the exhausting process of location scouting for *Straw Dogs*. Their search took them to the four corners of the British Isles.

I spent the next few weeks with him going all over the country looking for locations. We went to Scotland, Northern Ireland, Wales and ended up in Cornwall, which is where he found exactly what he wanted. And at certain points we would meet the producers along the way when we found something, and they would fly out, which is when I realised his jealousy.

We invited the producers to the hotel we were staying in. I said goodnight to everyone and went up to bed. Sam, who had been drinking, came up to my room, threw open the door and lambasted me, 'How dare you say goodnight to Dan Melnick [the film producer] first?'

I walked out on him that night and went straight back to London. It was quite a violent attack – not only verbal. That was when I learned what sort of relationship it was going to be.

But it wasn't just Katy who felt the keen edge of Peckinpah's unpredictable temper.

Frank Kowalski, [Sam's] continuity guy, they had a big row one night after they'd been drinking. Frank said, 'You're going to lose so many friends that you won't have enough people to carry your coffin to the grave.' A few days later they had another argument. Frank wrote a note and left it on Sam's bed: 'Exit one pall-bearer.'

When I first saw *Straw Dogs* I thought it looked a bit like a Hammer horror film, with Dustin Hoffman in the lead instead of Christopher Lee. It's certainly a flawed masterpiece. *Straw Dogs*, the world's first West Country western, was a movie with its own trouble budget built in. And that trouble was Peckinpah very nearly not finishing the film.

Mark Kermode describes one of the many 'events' that characterised the film's difficult production.

Very early on there was an event. Peck was enjoying himself, and went down to the coast to scream at the moon. He got pneumonia. She enabled him to finish it, shooting him in the thigh with B12, etc. Everyone agrees it was Katy who enabled *Straw Dogs* to get finished.

But love, like a pre-1972 Ford Capri with a double-barrelled carburettor, never runs smooth, and for Katy it was nothing short of an extended symphony of pain.

Sam met someone during pre-production on *Straw Dogs* who he later married. She came down to Cornwall. Her name was Joie Gould. That was difficult because he had a woman living with him while we were working.

Katy was still very much emotionally entangled with Peckinpah at that time.

Straw Dogs was finished and he got a commission to direct *Junior Bonner* in Prescott, Arizona. He packed up. He said goodbye to me, hoped we'd work together again if he came to England and he left!

Within three days I got a phone call. 'Get your ass over here; we've got a picture to make.'

Junior Bonner (1972), directed by Peckinpah and starring Steve McQueen, is one of the few Peckinpah films to have no gun violence in it. The story of a rodeo star facing an uncertain future, it seemed to touch his familiar themes of 'They've taken my job, destroyed my home, what have you done with the whiskey and this time I'm gonna teach you a lesson you'll never forget!' Once again Katy, at Peckinpah's side, was more than up to the challenge of making this sweet family movie.

That was a culture shock: a middle-class Jewish girl used to wearing Gucci shoes and Pucci nightdresses, stuck in the middle of a rodeo with Steve McQueen letting bulls out during the shoot. We had a great time – the only complication was getting drunken Indians out of jail each night so they could be on set in the morning. A happy set for a change.

During the making of Junior Bonner Katy caught a brief glimpse of Peckinpah's softer side.

There was a lot of his sadness for the loss of his father deeply ingrained in this film, and I saw another side of him which was kind, sweet and seductive. He did something wonderful when my mother's rented apartment came up for sale – he bought it for her. Very generous.

After such a mellow and touching film with only two violent scenes in it – a punch-up and a house demolition – you could be forgiven for thinking that maybe Peckinpah was beginning to settle down, pipe and slippers in hand, entering a golden age of acceptance and possibly even making a good woman out of Katy.

Unfortunately, a certain party had returned to this combustible mix . . . and was about to blow Katy's world apart.

At the end of filming [*Junior Bonner*] Sam said he was renting a condo in Studio City. 'All my stuff is in storage from Malibu from when I went to do *Straw Dogs*. Leave a week before the end of wrap and go and furnish the apartment.' His kids had packed up his house in Malibu in boxes, just piling stuff in – one box was his coffee table, including ashtrays and cigarettes. A nightmare!

Four days into it, Sam called and asked, 'How long are you going to be, because Joie and I have been living at the beach in a hotel waiting for you to finish the house.' I was dumbfounded.

In essence, Peckinpah's old lover Katy was furnishing a flat for him and his new lover Joie to move into.

I went back to England. A few weeks later I got a call saying, 'We've got *The Getaway* to shoot. Are you ready to come back?' I said, 'Sure!'

He and Joie were engaged, so I came back as a free agent. Little did I know I was also expected to be completely loyal.

The Getaway (1972), an inspiring heist-gone-horribly-wrong movie, starred Steve McQueen and his soon-to-be wife Ali MacGraw, who very quickly became friends with the twice-bitten, ready to be bitten again Katy.

We became friends because we were on location for *The Getaway*, which was as an understatement an exciting experience. She's so bright and she's funny and she's kind, so I immediately liked her and we became friends.

Did Peckinpah have a problem with Katy having female friends?

He didn't mind female relationships. Interesting question. But any other male in my life he couldn't handle.

Interestingly, Steve McQueen strikes Ali MacGraw in the film, making her the subject of Peckinpah's violence by proxy and him the first ever star to beat his wife-to-be on-screen. Ali remembers it well.

Sam looked up to Steve because Steve was larger than life at that point; an international icon for men, for women, young boys, girls. He was the whole thing.

Steve was a professional, so he wasn't giving me the level of slap that the camera take seems to suggest. I was swooning because I'm not someone who would stick around to have my face slapped. There are some who would allow that more than once. It was incredibly upsetting to film, and not something I'd do in real life.

Katy Haber, meanwhile, was quick to spot a pattern emerging in the way Peckinpah portrayed his lead women on-screen.

Women are punished. Sam adored women, but hated his reliance on and need for them. He needed and loved me, but resented that fact.

He would always say, 'We can't be together because the work is more important. I need to distance myself from you,' but he didn't allow me to distance myself from him.

Ali MacGraw agrees with Katy.

He thought that women were either ladies or whores – that old-fashioned, ill-educated judgement of what went into each.

And as if to prove the point, Peckinpah rubbed Katy's face in it all over again. In the middle of making *The Getaway* he and Joie went down to Juarez in Mexico and got married. Ali MacGraw recalls Katy's pain.

We talked about the hair-raising games that were played, and she didn't march off. There were days when it was wonderful, but then there was the bizarrely unkind behaviour of marrying someone before Katy knew this was on the horizon.

Katy wasn't allowed to leave her room even while the happy couple were tying the knot.

On the wedding night, I got a call to make sure I was in my room and on my own.

We finished the picture, and at the end Sam told me, 'Joie doesn't want you around. Now that we're married she feels you to be a threat.' I said, 'No problem, hope you'll be very happy.' And I went back to England again.

It was during this time that Katy got a call from a producer to work in Spain for another director called Sam, the legendary Sam Fuller, on the production of his new film based on his own short story 'Riata'. Mark Kermode is a fan of Fuller.

Sam Fuller is a great director. His films include *Naked Kiss*,

Big Red One . . . One of the auteurs of edgy cinema. A great poet of the cinema.

Katy couldn't believe she had been given an emotional break from Sam Peckinpah's unyielding, raging control. Unfortunately she found that while Fuller was a completely different kind of film-maker, he appeared to be hiring people rather familiar to Katy.

Having worked with Sam [Peckinpah], who I thought was a brilliant director, here I was working with another legend. I couldn't understand the legend – Fuller was a beginner. Interesting to work for a great director and realise how great the other director was.

What was interesting was that I was surrounded by Peckinpah people – Bo Hopkins from *The Wild Bunch*, Richard Harris from *Major Dundee*, and of all people, Alfonso Arau, [the bloodthirsty bandit] from *The Wild Bunch*. And the secretary was Sam's doctor's daughter. So I had this ghost of Peckinpah with me everywhere.

Katy had locked herself into a brutalising relationship with Sam Peckinpah regardless of where she went, a relationship set to loop and feedback with the Ernest Hemingway of directors. Relief came in the form of romance while she was working on the 'Riata' movie.

On this picture I met the most wonderful guy – a special-effects guy. After Peckinpah it was one of the greatest affairs of my life, but very short-lived. One of the most requited relationships I ever had. I was used to unrequited ones, like Sam. It was amazing, together every day on the picture. He was married with children, and I had a guilt complex.

Then the studio stepped in and made Fuller's film history.

Right in the middle of the film, Paramount said, 'This picture doesn't cut together'. Everyone was fired, so we all went home. I had to say goodbye, which was traumatic because I knew I'd never see him again.*

If that wasn't enough, Katy received the call again … to return to Peckinpah's side.

I got a phone call from Camille† to say that Sam and Joie had broken up. 'Sam is in Durango, Mexico, having a fit; knows that he's lost you. He's beside himself and wants to know if you know anyone who could come and work for him.'

Peckinpah even picked up the phone himself.

'Well,' he said, 'do you want to come back?'

'What are you talking about? You fired me, and Joie doesn't want me around.'

'Joie's gone.'

The trouble with Sam was, I so loved working with him that I accepted the emotional pain. I never should have mixed work with pleasure – there was always that dichotomy. The thought of him doing a picture without me was as painful as the fact that the other side wasn't working out. I came to terms with that.

Inevitably, she returned. The film this time was *Pat Garrett and Billy the Kid* (1973), starring James Coburn, Kris Kristofferson and Bob Dylan.

---

* The film was eventually completed as *The Deadly Trackers* (1973), under the directorship of Barry Shear.

† Camille Fielding, wife of composer Jerry Fielding, whose scores include *The Wild Bunch* and *Straw Dogs*.

About a week into *Pat Garrett and Billy the Kid*, the letters from my special-effects man stopped coming. I called the studio where he was working. He'd died the previous week. The last letter I'd had from him said, 'My heart is breaking, torn between holding your hand in one hand and my baby's hand in the other.' He died in his sleep and he was thirty-two. I was devastated and Sam wanted to know why I was so upset. 'Why didn't you tell me?' he said. I said, 'Why would I want to tell you that the man I love has died?' He acted in a compassionate way, which was an interesting reaction.

The drink and the lifestyle were catching up with Peckinpah. His next film, *Killer Elite* (1975), a karate flick about CIA hit men starring Robert Duvall, was a mess, but the main problem was drugs: there simply weren't enough of them.

It was an era when drugs were part of the production budget. This was the seventies.

Mark Kermode finds it incredible that so many great movies were made during this time.

If you read about this period of movies made between 1968 and 1975 – and we are talking about some of the greatest works of US cinema, like *Easy Rider* and *Raging Bull* – how was anything ever made with so many people working on them in advanced states of refreshment?

No doubt by straight-headed people who cleared up the mess to get the job finished. People like Katy.

By now Peckinpah was in an almost permanent state of chemical assistance – hardly ideal when piloting big-budget films. So distorted was his thinking that he deluded himself into a substitution.

He really felt that he had conquered his dependency by giving up drinking and transferring his addiction to cocaine. It made him impossible. It was the beginning of the end of our relationship.

It got to the point where the studios couldn't deal with Sam. I became the barrier, the battering ram. I always came out with the answers. I was able to manipulate him into working if he was drunk or whatever. Sometimes he would not come onto the set until five o'clock in the afternoon. With drinking, at least he was sober in the morning, but with cocaine he was much more angry.

Ali MacGraw remembers vividly the difference between the director's various states of addiction and how they affected Katy.

The level of cruelty got so baroque that it escalated into an exhibitionism of meanness, almost begging to be busted. I often think, what would have happened if she'd come through with a frying pan and cold-cocked him? Would he have gone, 'Wow, that's some old lady I have'? There are all these weak, cornball directions for how to be a real man, and I think he subscribed to all of them.

Katy's next Peckinpah project was *Cross of Iron* (1977), starring James Coburn.

That was a great film to make because it was James Coburn and we were all very close friends.

We were shooting under terrible conditions, wearing masks all the time because we were burning tyres. We had a Yugoslavian crew, who had all been in the Resistance during the war, and a German producer who ran around telling everyone he had been in the Panzer division in the Second World War and had the bullets in his arse to prove it. So you had Sam and the crew paying the producer back for World War II, doing a movie about the German soldiers on the Russian front.

On a whim, she, Peckinpah and Coburn decided to flee the acrid hellhole of a Yugoslav film set for nearby Venice. Just for the day. That same day another director was in town.

Coburn and I met downstairs. I went up to get Sam and he said he didn't want to go out – he just wanted to sleep. Back in the lobby, Federico Fellini walks in. He and Coburn hugged and Fellini said, 'Xchamess Coburn, how are you?' You can be in the film business and work with Dustin Hoffman and Steve McQueen, but there are certain people who walk into your life and leave you gob-smacked. Fellini's one of them: you don't meet people like Fellini very often.

Coburn introduced us. I said, 'Maestro, there's someone upstairs I want you to meet.' I took him up, knocked on the door and Sam said, 'What?'

'Sam, there's someone out here that I want you to meet.'

He used a word I can't say. I persisted, and eventually he opened the door completely naked. 'Sam Peckinpah, Federico Fellini.'

Sam said, 'Oh . . . my . . . God.'

Fellini said, 'Sam Peckinpah,' and threw his arms round the naked man. They went in the room and Sam poured some brandy. Coburn and I spent hours in Venice doing things, and when we got back about four in the afternoon they were in exactly the same spot. Who knows what they talked about?

One of Peckinpah's final big-budget films proved to be his undoing. *Convoy* (1978), inspired by C. W. McCall's chart-topping hit of three years earlier, was a poor movie that did nothing for Peckinpah's career and, it seemed, even less for Katy's relationship with him, as Ali MacGraw recalls.

It was ugly and over, and Katy was gone by the middle of the film. That was the film where Sam's disease was out of control. The substances he used to anaesthetise his demons had changed because of physical repercussions. He had elected to drink 'just champagne with a side hit of a little cocaine'. He was very erratic.

Katy found her ex-lover now beyond tolerable to be with or work for.

The film was difficult to make because it was a bad script. Sam was very much into cocaine and difficult to work with. Sam fired me off *Convoy*. That was all to do with jealousy. He moved in with the woman whose house he was renting, and I said, 'Screw this – enough already.' I had an affair with the cameraman, and Sam found out and couldn't stand it.

I found a bug in the hotel room, and I was paying for the room next door where someone was listening in on me. That's how Sam's paranoia was getting out of hand.

I found the bug and confronted Sam with it, saying, 'This is ridiculous.'

Ali MacGraw remembers the bug incident.

Katy was convinced that Sam had bugged the room. I looked at her incredulously – that is endgame cocaine craziness, if it were true. I dare say it was possible. He was paranoid.

Whatever, Katy was no longer part of the *Convoy* shoot.

I was fired, came back to England and never spoke to him

again. He died five years later and I was pissed because we really hadn't sorted the problem out.

Katy went on to work on many more motion pictures, this time being given appropriate credit for her work. She worked with Michael Deeley and Michael Cimino on *The Deerhunter* (1978) and was a producer of *Blade Runner* (1982) and several other titles.

For those of my generation who grow misty-eyed thinking of Ridley Scott's masterpiece, having 'Producer, *Blade Runner*' on one's CV would represent a career pinnacle. But for Katy the grotesque, bathetic and brutal relationship she endured dominates her professional achievements like a great beast that refuses to lie down.

It was the most emotional, the pivotal time in my life. Whatever I'm doing now, my relationships all reflect back on those eight years. Talking about it puts a lump in my throat. It was the most important eight years of my life.

He was the most fascinating, the most debilitating, seductive and amazing person to be around. Take all the negatives and positives and put them in a barrel, you can't possibly give it up and you can't regret it. But it was not normal.

It's an integral part of my life, and I consider it like a marriage. I resent the fact that because of that I never had children and never married anybody else – those were my child-bearing years.

Mark Kermode is in no doubt about Katy's true purpose in continuing the relationship.

People were amazed as to why she was hanging out with Peck. He used to throw bowie knives at the wall. He was armed. And there he was in the presence of this erudite person. No one has a bad word to say about her. He was the mad, out-of-control guy and she was the firm hand on the tiller.

Peckinpah is seen in a 1970 documentary about the making of *Straw Dogs* actually throwing knives at a wall. Even when he lived with Katy he was quick on the draw.

I got up in the middle of the night, and when I emerged from the bathroom a bullet clipped my ear and landed in the doorway. Sam had forgotten I was there and fired on me because he thought I was an intruder. I was none too pleased.

Ali MacGraw speculates on Katy's relationship with him.

I'm not sure that if Sam had just been a wonderful plumber that she met she would have put up with all of this. She's attracted to renegade, go-against-the-system dreamers, and they all have a side which winds up hurting her and messing with her self-esteem, so the question is, 'Does she have any?'

Inevitably they flip over the charm and start again, and she's like a hungry little puppy, so grateful for that biscuit. It's terrifying as a girlfriend to watch it.

But as it went on over the years, one has to think two people signed up for that dance.

Since the endless summers of Sam Peckinpah, Katy has been active for BAFTA in Los Angeles and works with the homeless, but Ali MacGraw is in no doubt about her remarkable contribution to both Peckinpah's work and to other great films.

She's worked for some extraordinary contributors to twentieth-century film, and made a difference in some major movies. She's had an interesting life so far, and the night is young.

In fact, Mark Kermode is convinced that without Katy there would be no later Sam Peckinpah films at all.

It wouldn't be completely fanciful to say she was the co-director. She was allowing the director to direct.

Katy Haber remains in the film business and is firm friends with Ali MacGraw, but she has had her life effectively defined by one man's artistic endeavours. This is, after all, the story of a woman who devoted all of her child-rearing years to looking after one: Sam Peckinpah.

10

I Was Johnny Cash's Tailor

In 1957 two things happened: I made a gold lamé suit for Elvis Presley, and then I started making clothes for Johnny Cash.

Nashville is a busy, commercially significant city in America's South and not the poor one it's sometimes taken for. Pictures of great country-and-western stars beam down at you from the walls of the airport lobby; seasoned country legends, veterans of the Grand Ole Opry, every performer adorned in the dazzling uniform of the genre: shirts with collar studs, rhinestone-packed waistcoats, skintight tops with frills or ruffles in a range of bright cheerful colours, together with blue, brown or red diamond-studded jackets, cowboy hats and boots to match, all exclusive to this magical if sugar-coated wishing well of the music world. But one performer disdained the sartorial razzamatazz: Johnny Cash – the original Man in Black.

A star of Nashville and an icon of American song, Johnny Cash was a singer for whom black was always the new black, like Burt Lancaster's Elmer Gantry with a chip on one shoulder and a guitar slung over the other.

Manuel Cuevas, a gifted, hard-working designer of distinctive clothing, could see the 'metaphysical' black in Johnny Cash and was the performer's first tailor.

He met Cash in 1956. After a lengthy apprenticeship with Nudie Cohn – the architect of the Wild Bill Hickok cowboy fashions a generation earlier – Manuel had just hit the big time by designing an outfit for Elvis Presley.

Manuel is the self-styled 'King of Cowboy Bling'. His shop at 1922 Broadway, Nashville, is a complete, self-contained fashion business. It is world renowned.

As I walk into the ground-floor showroom I spot J. D. Souther, singer-songwriter, briefly one of the Eagles and backing vocalist on Randy Newman's great 'cowboy' song 'Rider in the Rain'. He is there to pick out some clothes and take some advice from Manuel.

Upstairs, on the second floor, is the 'foundry' of his business. His cheerful staff are cutting patterns, fabric is carefully being checked and finished and designs sketched out for clients. This is definitely a family-friendly fashion concern. Everyone is engaged on some aspect of the job, either sewing rhinestones to sleeves, cutting cloth or making coffee for up-and-coming country singers waiting to be fitted for a stage costume downstairs. Manuel's office is crowded with outfits and gifts from his clients. Manuel has an incredible speaking voice; a complex, beautiful medley of south-western American and Mexican phrasing, with a confident tone and a gift for well-chosen metaphors that sum up clients, clothes, people, the business he is in and his part in it. He showed me some of his famous outfits. He showed me the guitar Johnny Cash had given him as a present. Then we settled down to talk about his client as a young man.

*

John is a young man, as is Johnny Mathis, as is Kris Kristofferson, as is Willie Nelson, as is Roger Miller. All of them were growing up at the same time, and that was back in 1956.

In 1957 two things happened: I made a gold lamé suit for Elvis Presley, and then I started making clothes for Johnny Cash. 'I Walk the Line' was his hit at that particular time.

We enjoyed a friendship with each other, and with others that I already mentioned, and we were kids hanging out like the normal barrio people. I was apparently always single, so most of them just hung at my place, and I always had a nice homey-type home. If you want to say that you had been in my house, then you kind of had to piss on the floor and wipe your – you know – as you fly out the window. That's the kind of very friendly, very giving camaraderie.

But then the sparkle, the career, starts for Johnny Cash, and he says, 'You know, I have a lot of shows lined up, and I think we have it. So I want you to make me nine suits. I calculated you should make me nine suits to start this career.'

I said, 'Well, good.'

'We are doing this like in a hurry.'

'No big deal. I will work day and night and will get 'em together.'

So I went ahead, cut 'em, made 'em up and sent them to him. And then who do I hear on the phone but Johnny Cash.

He says, 'Manuel, I got my suits.'

I said, 'Yes, John?'

'Nine of them.'

I said, 'Yeah, nine. That's what you ordered. Nine.'

'How come they are all black?'

I said, 'John, there is something that I think you should try. There is some sort of eminency that you make through your persona, something I cannot describe, but it's definitely sinister in a way. You look good in black.'

'Well, I guess I'm going to try it for a while.'

Since 1957 to two or three years ago, Johnny never ordered anything in any other colour. So the press and people said, 'Oh, Manuel made Johnny Cash the Man in Black.' And one time we had a little interview and he said, 'Well, I could say that I wore black before, but then Manuel put me in a better black.'

Manuel's amazing skill was in making these nine monochrome suits individually distinctive, with different patterns, stitching, cuts and fabric for each. You can have any colour you like, John, so long as it's black.

I made a Johnny Cash style. Straight yokes, very simplified, but nevertheless tailored and cut properly. So he didn't only look sinister. His charisma; it's like he could part the water. The way I saw Johnny Cash at the beginning was a young boy singing country music of his own kind. And if that's not captivating then what is? I knew John would make it big, because he had that seriousness, that privacy and that sainthood. He was a very sinister human being, but captivating like you have no idea.

I was born in Mexico about seventy-four years ago, and I started sewing when I was seven years old. A total accident, because I had a brother playing with tailoring, and he kind of forced me to sit down on one of the sewing machines and help him. And I never left the machine, but he definitely disappeared from tailoring. We all were, you know, normal people. We went to school, to college, got a degree. But I continued with the tailoring all my life, to this day, and after graduating and doing whatever I've done in my life – which is so many things – I stuck to the designing and the tailoring.

And it has become my castle, where I get inspired, where I develop whatever it is that people like out there. I just make clothes. I learned bootmaking, shoemaking, jewellery; anything that has to do with the horse and rider too, like saddles, like belts, like bags, purses for ladies, dresses, gowns.

The thing about being a designer, it bores you if you start doing the same thing. I was making now, my God, ninety to a hundred and ten gowns a year for all the proms and the receptions, sweet sixteens, marriages and all that, and some fancy girls that wanted to get dressed by a designer. And all that was fine, but it was too much of the same. That's the reason I moved to Los Angeles when I was twenty-one.

I fell right in the middle of Hollywood. So I got to do all the suits for Frank Sinatra, for all the Rat Pack from Las Vegas, and comedians like Bob Hope, Joey Bishop and Jerry Lewis. I was searching for a niche. I was making incredible money doing all these suits for these guys, and the tipping was outstanding.

But, you know, you need food for the soul; you don't need food for the table any more after you buy whatever you need. I said, 'Well, where am I going?' And I went to see the Rose Parade in Pasadena and that fascinated me. I thought, 'This is what I should be doing: flamboyancy, things that really shine, that glitter.'

'Who makes these clothes?' I asked my girlfriend.

She says, 'Well, there's two people. There's one person on Ventura Boulevard, there's another person on Vineland Avenue. The one on Vineland is Nudie Cohn. And Nudie's is a rodeo tailor store where they sell western stuff. This is special apparel.'

I said, 'Well, I was looking at all the other things.'

'Oh,' she says. 'Well, this other man, on Ventura Boulevard, has dressed a lot of people and put a lot of rhinestones. All these designs – I don't know where they come from.'

'Well, that's just American history. It's good stuff.'

So I went to see Mr [Nathan] Turk. And he looked at me, checked me out, but he didn't give me a job. I wanted a place where I could just do something, create something.

He actually had his son-in-law in there, so when he said no, I kind of liked that. I said, 'OK.' I'm not going to interfere with anybody. I really want to kind of go in and take over.

I went to Nudie, and Nudie said that he would hire me. He was in a very difficult situation one day; I helped him out with some tailoring, and he says, 'You mean you can cut?' And I said, 'Yes. I can do more than that.'

He hired me, and all of a sudden I had to hire my own people because he fired everybody. He just liked my style, and if you go through the catalogues of Nudie, then you find out exactly when I show up in the catalogue. And then things start getting like a little kid playing with rhinestones and embroidery.

The history of American fashion has its roots in the clothing worn by the Pilgrim Fathers, those Europeans who joined them, their descendants, the tough western pioneers and homesteaders and, most importantly, the original inhabitants of the New World who were slowly marginalised by the settlers. The designs, colours and styles of the clothing worn by the many different Native American tribes were adopted by some white European immigrants, especially in the west. For Manuel these Indian motifs and icons had particular significance and inspired his imagination as a designer.

Because of my studies, being a nerd, I had already a minor in American History. I loved the history; not only of the Lone Ranger, but also Tonto. You always face history, wherever you go, and I just wanted to know more and more and more and more. To the point where most of the stuff – well, not most of it, I should say all of it – that I do, I use Indian signs that are real.

I am very familiar with Indian history. So even the wording of some sayings that I have put on so many pieces, it's very genuine, very real. And the same with the cowboy, the settlers, the old-time stuff. It's not because I lived as long as Santa Claus, it's because I like the theme. I can't help it; I was born in North America. I know nothing *but* American style, the heritage that we have from the Incas to the Cheyenne. We extend from end to end, from Canada, from Alaska to Patagonia, so we have all that.

It's fascinating, because when the European horse married the Indian in America, it was the greatest way of transportation for them. And that's why Indians became the greatest riders in the world. First of all, they didn't need a saddle for that. This is the way they thought the Spaniards were. They thought the horse and the person were just one person moving; they couldn't separate. It was later on, I think early 1600s, when they started putting horse blankets and weaving them instead of a saddle. I go back into that history. I've been digging it all the time.

It was difficult for Manuel not to find the cowboy chic left in the trail of Wild Bill Hickok's Travelling Western Tales getting in the way of his fashion voice. Strangely, it was in the entertainment industry itself that Manuel's inspiration began.

I have one designer I have admired all my life. I just love this designer. I entered the movie industry in 1956, when I did *Giant*. Miss Edith Head could see in me my future somehow. She said, 'Manuel, you are the King of the Cowboys. You really know how to do this, how to do that, how to block a hat, how to make everything from chaps to scarves.'

She really admired me, and she said, 'You know, I hope that one day when I'm gone you take possession of the studios here.'

'Well, that will be a little too ambitious for me.'

'No, it's not. Let me introduce you to this kid.' And this kid was sewing with his face to the wall, and he says his name is Bob Mackie. 'This guy is going to be a great designer one day,' and true enough, later on I heard about him.

I had the chance and the opportunity to work with her in so many movies and so many wardrobes. And whenever a horse walked into her place, she called me and said, 'Man, I got something for you.'

I did so many westerns, like Marshal Dillon [*Gunsmoke*], *Bonanza* for fourteen years, *Big Valley*, *Tolly*, *High Chaparral*, *The Lancers*, *Dallas* and what have you; so many of those things.

It was because I know how to read the character. Once they give me the script, I can get it going. I think since I had worked momentarily on *Rawhide*, and I kind of knew Clint Eastwood, I got this script from Sergio Leone. He said, 'I'm making some westerns.' And it was a little strange for me to see an Italian producing westerns, but apparently somebody told him to call me or get me involved. They said, 'The Man from Nowhere – this guy is a man that is from nowhere.' So I had to find a personality for him, and that's how his wardrobe started that he ended up using all his life. And he is known more for that than any other thing, although he has won Oscars and things.

When you think of the Clint Eastwood character, you think of a poncho, the hat, the cigar. Very, very simple, like Gaucho meets Portuguese cattle rustler and Habitat tea cosy. But this is not the way to be thinking.

I made sure that nobody could identify the poncho as Serape, as Mexican, or Navajo. It was definitely from the Americas, the blanket, but I made sure that nobody could identify it.

Manuel styled Clint Eastwood in all of his spaghetti westerns.

I'm telling you, I date back to the Bible.

He styled Johnny Cash for quite a few films too.

John never changed. He could play a character, of course he could, but you never lost Johnny Cash in the movie. They could never have done that, the movie-makers, even if they shaved his hair, because John's presence came from way deep. You could put an Indian costume on the man, but you will never see the costume, you just feel John.

Because John was the man: the Man in Black.

I drive almost every Sunday to my shop because my church is at the corner. So I am getting out of my car and I feel this presence, you know. He's sitting on the grass, on the railroad tracks there, and I see these long legs. As I followed, there's Johnny Cash, and he says, 'Brother, do you always arrive this late at work in the morning?'

And I say, 'Johnny Cash, do you realise it's Sunday? And I'm going to *church*. I didn't come to work.'

'Well, I would like to sit down and talk with you about things.'

Cash was going through many personal trials at the time.

Of course, I cannot make comments about those things – very private things, very nice things. But always we had the time to discuss life, which is very important.

All those personal things he really solved by himself. There was no way in the world that I could tell him what I tell my brother Marty Stuart. He was very private. He had his tasks with his soul. You could see him thinking, but instead of worrying about him, you wanted to be like him. You know what I mean?

He just had that thing. He would go to the mountain or to the cave; all those stories are true. It was just John and himself, finding himself and struggling, dealing with the fusion between him and drugs and what have you.

There was some tension when Manuel left Nathan Turk to set up on his own.

When I went on my own, John was angry because I didn't call him. I said, 'John, I don't want to take clientele from my ex-boss or anything like that.'

'No,' he said, 'but you're my tailor and you are going to remain my tailor. And we're also friends, we're also brothers.' He was very clear with me on that. 'I need clothes right now. I want you to come to my show tonight. I'm at the sports arena and I want to see you.'

'John, OK, I will go and I will see you.'

'Well, come early because we get busy when the show starts,' meaning go backstage and see him.

He's getting his make-up done. He can see me coming in the hallway, and he said, 'Here comes my friend Manuel and I'm going to have a talk with him.' And all these people start marching out of the room.

'I've never been so happily embarrassed, John. Why did you throw . . . ?'

'I never said anything, Manuel.'

I remember one of his entourage throwing the door open. 'Have a nice chat, Manuel.'

I said, 'Come on!'

'I never said for them to leave.' But that was the kind of man he was. You could feel the presence. You know what? I respect his singing and everything he did. I think his presence inspired me more than anything.

He was a saint. He was a spirit in the most profound way.

The way that I could describe Johnny Cash is, I think, my brother had more spirit than a monk. He probably makes a monk look like a joker, because he was very serious. And he would be serious with me and with everybody. You know, not a guy that just chats and bulls, no, no, no. He could do that, but his words were beautifully chosen. John would possess you when he was talking.

First of all, he knew how to treat his friends, which is something very admirable in a person, but he was always the same person. He remained the same human being to everybody. And no matter what they did, no matter what happened, forget all those fun times, he was always the guy that was very serious. He knew how to conduct himself.

One of the most brilliant men I have ever known. I think he is probably on top of my list. He sat here many times. I can feel his presence, his guitar is right there. He gave me a beautiful guitar.

To many who knew him and saw him, Johnny Cash had the spiritual presence of a preacher, a preacher of music, and when he was in the room they were transfixed by him. It fascinated me that Manuel could disconnect himself from the great brooding presence to measure this preacher's inside leg.

It's difficult trying to hold down a codpiece when you're surrounded by so many temptations. Was Cash ever 'unfaithful' to another tailor?

Not that I know, but if there was . . . how great. But I never saw him with anything else but my clothes. [*Laughs*]

The signature was there.

Yes, kind of. It was no longer my signature; it was Johnny Cash's signature. This is what I tell everybody: if you don't have an image, I'm sorry, you can make money, but you're never going to make it within yourself, with your crafts-manship, with your personality, with your soul. Anybody can make money, but an image; all you had to do is see a *shadow* of Johnny Cash, and you know that's Johnny Cash.

Manuel made a staggering number of outfits for Cash.

To my surprise, I saw the big sale in Sotheby's; they sent me a book. One of his suits sold for sixty-five or sixty-nine thousand. I only made five thousand out of that one. But anyway. [*Laughs*] It's just like crazy, isn't it? I did so many things. When I saw that book I could not believe it. All of the dresses that June [Carter Cash] had were my dresses. All of the jackets and pants, dusters, anything . . . it was my stuff. For that alone I am so grateful.

Did Cash put Manuel under a lot of pressure when it came to suits?

Oh yes, that happened many times. But not in design – he always let me do whatever. I did a lot of acorn designs, because to me he's like an oak tree, but always with the inspiration of a strong character. He loved the Indian life of America, and I did a lot of that stuff for him. Those were like sacred things for him; Indian signs, Indian themes. I did a prairie with Indians showing up on horses. There were some roses sometimes, and things like that, but it was black on black on black, so you had to be like a foot away from John to identify the stuff.

John got his clothes and he'll be on the phone: 'Great suits, Manuel. I really like this.' That type of clientele is hard to find. If he did it because of our friendship, then I'm more gratified. I mean, I never want to step out of bounds, but when you are their designer, you know their soul.

Was Johnny Cash's style inspired by the fact that religious figures, priests and so on, wore robes?

I think I made him look like a minister sometimes, like some kind of religious personality, but a little more powerful; like a sage, like some kind of shaman. He was the rock or the spirit, the mountain, the unclimbable mountain.

As a tailor with a spiritual dimension, Manuel clearly has a great talent for spotting the real person behind the insecure patina of some artist clients.

It happens to a lot of artists. Sometimes they dress superwell, and next day they are walking around with regular clothes, or sweats. Johnny Cash was not that type of person.

Manuel has a simple rule of thumb when eyeing up potential clients looking for showbiz costumes with a massive advance in their back pockets after signing to a big record company.

Well, you've got to meet 'em, but you have to listen to their music. They are musicians. Others come from other walks of life, and again you need to *know* these people in order to find an image for them. I have so many people that have the money to buy clothes, and to buy whatever, but they get absolutely tired of having the same suit that the other guy is wearing at the same party. They don't want to be ridiculed. There's a certain kind of pride out there, you know, which I am all blessed with, because I'll tell you what, that keeps bread on *my* table. So these people order clothes from me and they say, 'Can you just find me?' And I do. I see the way they act, the way they do their thing, and it's easy for me to dress the gambler, the beggar, the prostitute, the saint, the priest, the clown, the king, the queen.

You cannot hide from Manuel. He can see the inner soul of every performer.

Yes, I learned to do that. I don't know why – my background, from my uncle being a great philosopher, my parents being superb people and raising kids and all that . . . all these things. I was kind of a soul guy.

And when it came to studies, I was a nerd, so just imagine. Put those two together!

OK. I want one. Just to wear in the house or occasionally to a wedding to show everyone I'm authentic. Name your price, pardner!

I would say a normal suit will start at two thousand five hundred dollars.

That's very reasonable.

Yes. I always remained that way. What I really sell is uniqueness. I only make one of a kind. I never repeat anything for anybody.

It's not about selling clothes. It's not about making suits every day. It's not about somebody looking good and they happen to have one of my suits. No, all I want is for them to look beautiful and to look acceptable.

But the thing that fascinates me the most in anything that anybody on this earth wears is something that fits their character. Something that tells your friends, your mom, your dad, strangers who you are.

I finally summoned up the courage to ask him: how would you go about dressing a dishonest person . . . like me?

I dress them very dishonest. What are you going to do, man? You see the bad side too, you know. There's different dark sides. There are dark sides that are red and silver and gold. You got to do it. You *got* to do it.

And they are so happy. This is what I want. You know the guys that say in the street language, 'This is badass!' I say, 'Well, yeah.' And I love it because it *suits* them.

So many ladies that I've dressed, they said, 'What do you think I should look like, because I like short skirts?'

I said, 'Well, let me tell you one thing. The difference between a lady and a prostitute is probably a half an inch in the length of the skirt. So let's be very careful how we do this.'

And all of a sudden they discover that. When you bend down to pick up your purse, are you taking pictures or are you *being taken* by the camera? You gotta understand that. You need to know: are you the object? [*Laughs*]

So you're in the sordid trade of selling people an image of themselves that is exactly the one they're projecting anyway.

I am never taken by fashion or trends. I want that person to look her- or himself. That's all I want. I'm not talking about how many layers here, or the length of this, or the length of that, or whatever. I am going for the personality. And man, I am so lucky and I just get it. It's a gift.

Of course, I get people that bring me pictures and say, 'I want something like this.' And I recommend them to another tailor. I think it's fun.

Manuel is a legend. The designer Oscar de la Renta believes Manuel makes classic clothes that remain important despite the changing fashions.

Actually I was eavesdropping on an interview that he was having, but I was no more than three feet away from him, so I could not avoid it. The interviewer says, 'And what do you think about Manuel?'

He says, 'Well, Manuel is another breed. Because while we are doing our fashion, breaking our heads about what everybody's going to wear in forty-five days or three months, during all this time that we are killing ourselves, judging the design and the look for the next season, Manuel is patiently hand-sewing a suit for a client. A suit that is going to be around for the next thirty-five years.'

Oscar is a great guy, but we are not super-friends or anything like that. But we recognise each other, and I respect everybody.

How long was I going to have to wait for my cowboy crooning costume – days, weeks, months?

Several. When I have a concept, I don't have the full concept. I start; it's very much like sketching. When I am doing my drawings, which is every day, I think I use more the eraser than the pencil, honestly, because that right-hand side of the brain has to work. You have to find new things. And maybe that's what keeps me alive, what gives me feeling. It gives me a better spirit.

I love new things. The kids who come to intern with me, and I have ten of them all the time, I love that because they teach me so many new things. And yet they come here so I can teach *them*.

Man, I learn from the fools and I learn from the intelligent, I learn from the wise.

Manuel has a massive library of designs after so many years of making outfits for the stars. He doesn't need to steal anyone else's ideas. He can simply steal his own.

I tell my students, 'We're going to do pieces in similar style to what I used to do fifty years ago.' They look at me like it's a joke. These kids are twenty years old.

I say, 'Listen, I have an open mind. Over here we have no bodies and we have no eyes, all we have is open minds. So when it comes to dress the body, we look, we think, we create. We're not looking at breasts; we're not looking at waistlines. We're not looking at fat people, or thin people, at perfect people or imperfect people. We are looking at design and we're creating.

'Forget what you like. Forget what you would wear. Be a fashionista, love everything. Love every button, every piece of fabric. You can make a suit out of wood, and you can make it out of wool, and you can make it out of tin cans.

'Be creative, be open-minded, and go there.'

That's my main ambition, to teach them and to let them know everything I think I know.

There's humility at the core of what Manuel does. It fills the room like a moonstone-studded air bag that will never deflate because it is bursting at the seams with his talent.

I remember very well a shirt that I was doing for Salvador Dalí. And he says, 'What is precisely this design, young man?'

And I said, 'Well, that is the Hispanic flower.'

'I don't recall seeing any flower like this before. Where exactly do they grow?'

'Right here, in the brain.'

He just gave me the eye, and I loved that man. I knew ten thousand times more about him than he knew about me.

I'm glad to see that some of those pieces are in the Smithsonian, and I love that stuff. It gives me the creeps, to tell you the truth, but it gives me the cold chills when I go into the Rock & Roll Hall of Fame Museum and see ZZ Top and all those stars, and pieces from God knows who. Sometimes I pass them. Sometimes I rediscover them.

More than about four or five times, I think, it's happened to me now that I see pieces where I've had to do a double check, and, 'Yes, I made them.'

That is really amazing. It's very fortifying for me.

An astonishing feeling to have, isn't it? 'Did I make that? Yes, I did. I did make that. I made that.' Like an old friend who simply won't leave you alone but who you always like to be around anyway.

It's incredible. Some guy who's thirty-five, forty years old says, 'You know, I have the suit that you made for my father. It's my favourite suit. I wear it only on super occasions.' It's so gratifying.

I dressed so many people, so many, especially the rock 'n' rollers. Maybe my life with the cowboy scene has been more caught by the press, but I made things for the Rolling Stones, I made pieces for the Beatles, I made things for the Jackson Five. I dressed them for years and years. And the Osmond brothers I am *still* dressing – since they were little babies. The Bee Gees, Earth, Wind and Fire, the Riders of the Purple Sage, the Grateful Dead, all those.

Manuel designed outfits for Gram Parsons, the Eagles and many others.

Dolly Parton. Linda Ronstadt; all her life I have dressed her. Songwriters from all walks of life. John David Souther has been my friend from years and years; we go back to Moses.

They say, 'Oh, you did the emblem for the Grateful Dead?'

I say, 'No, I did not.' I *did* the skeletons, because, of course, it's the Grateful *Dead*.

I was flying, I was on the plane thinking, 'What am I going to do for the Grateful Dead?' Well, hello? El Día de los Muertos. Grateful. Happy. Blah blah blah. Yeah.

John Lennon says, 'I want my first American western suit.' You know what I did? Black on black on black, and he says, 'What am I, Johnny Cash?'

I said, 'After taxes.' He just laughed and cracked about that, but he was very proud. I knew that he wanted a western suit, but in no way he wanted piping and rawhide. We're talking about a young Englishman, you know. Another sinister guy that also loved to converse with me.

I have this knack about these people; they don't talk to other people, they talk to me. Marlon Brando was the same way. John Lennon was exactly the same way. And you know, from the Beatles, George Harrison was hardly mingling. He talked to me, and I loved it because he was always an Englishman, so British. I loved him. There was some seriousness about him that I really loved.

And the same with Bob Dylan. I've dressed him, I would say, twenty-five years – I don't want to make him too old. After all, Bob would not appreciate that. He is another person that is very short on the talk, but when he comes, he visits me, we talk *a lot*.

'And when are you going to make me a *real* Manuel suit?' he says.

I say, 'I just don't want to ruin your career, that's why.'

John Lennon told me, 'Aren't you lucky you had Jimi Hendrix playing guitar in your yard?'

I said, 'John, it gets as simple as that. We're all human beings. We all do the normal thing, and it's fun to enjoy people of all walks of life. That stardom that you guys go for, it's thrilling and it's fantastic, because I've seen you guys nervous.'

Me, I never get nervous. When I'm with the beggar or with one of the presidents of this country – I made clothes for three or four of them – I feel just very simple.

I did for [George] Walker Bush, I did for his father. I did for Ronald Reagan for so many years; as an actor, as a lawyer, as a governor, and as a president, which is quite a fantastic thing.

He was so proud when he was going to China. This knock came into my store, and I turn around and I said, 'Oh, what a great honour, Mr President.' He says, 'Cut the crap, Manuel.'

That was a natural thing coming from me. I am never impressed by anybody. The Dalai Lama is a good example. He said to me, 'I think you're too commercial.' I meet people of all walks of life, and to wait five minutes to see the Dalai Lama was an eternity to me. It was like lining up for bread in Russia two hundred years ago. Come on, give me a break!

I have been one of the luckiest fellows.

Manuel can lay claim to giving the great John Travolta his first ever brush with rhinestone.

When John Travolta and Debra Winger were doing their thing, they thought I was going to make a lot of real fancy stuff for them. Debra, who was an old friend, had made a promise that when she made it into the movies she was going to introduce me to very important people.

She called me and she said, 'Do you know John Travolta?'

I said, 'No.' I had made some costumes for the guy, but if I'm doing works for commercials or a movie, I was handed always the name of the character, not the artist; because they don't want to excite you, I guess or whatever. I could care less, you know?

They came in and I said, 'John, nice meeting you.'

And he looks at me straight in the eye, and he wouldn't take his eyes off me. 'Sir,' he says, 'you're my hero.'

'Yeah, and my name is Santa Claus, right?'

'Seriously, sir, you are my hero.'

'And precisely where does that come from?'

He says, 'I was a little boy, and I walked into Nudie's with my mother. She was buying me a little felt hat that used to be a dollar seventy-nine or something like that, and you asked me if I was a cowboy.'

'Yes, I remember.'

'And you gave me a rhinestone tie, and this rhinestone scarf is hanging on my headboard right now in my house, and I want you to please come and check it out.'

So I did.

Life puts you, just like it's put me, with the right people at the right time at the right place. I mean, how lucky can I get? I do what I really love to do, because I love the cloth. I love it with a passion. It probably is my number-one liking, really, in my life. And then I get paid for it. I think it's so great. It's just fantastic. It's a beautiful merry-go-round.

II

I Was Dudley Moore's
First Bandleader

PREVIOUS PAGE
John Bassett (right) with Dudley Moore

'What larks eh, Pip? What larks!'
Joe Gargery in *Great Expectations* by Charles Dickens

Dudley Moore, one of the greatest musical comedians, jazz pianists and composers of the twentieth century, key member of the sixties satirist movement and star of such Hollywood blockbusters as *10* and *Arthur*, was born in Dagenham on 19 April 1935. From an early age he showed prodigious musical talent, and while at grammar school was encouraged by his piano teacher to apply for a music scholarship to Oxford or Cambridge. To his surprise, one of his applications was successful, and he became the organ scholar of Magdalen College in 1959. At Oxford he came into contact with fellow student John Bassett, a trumpeter with a love of jazz and big bands who had assembled several groups at the University Cellars, a club established by a fellow undergraduate who would later become deputy prime minister: Michael Heseltine. Moore's scholarship and the requirement it placed on him to play the Magdalen College organ meant that he spent much time at the keyboard.

In the mid-fifties John Bassett was heading for Oxford University to study Architecture, but was first obliged, like most young men in those days, to complete two years' national service with the armed forces. He chose to join the Royal Navy Blue Jackets band in Portsmouth, where marching to and from the ship could be a hazardous practice.

*

Trumpet players are positioned at the back of the band because you have to have your elbows up, parallel to the ground, so you can't see it, and you have the music in front of you on a small card on which you're concentrating. The only way to know where you're going is to watch the feet of the people either side of you. When you're marching companies either to or from the ship across the dockyard, you trip over rails, coils of wire, holes in the ground, and thereby a lot of trumpeters lose their teeth.

Unlike most people in the services who say 'never volunteer', I found that if you volunteered for something that caused you absolutely no hardship whatsoever the officers were so astounded, they gave you the most enormous rewards. I had been on HMS *Perseus*, on the anchor deck, where it was dirty, chain mud – there's nowhere for the mud to go. So I volunteered to play the bugle as the boat docked in Malta, Cairo, Yemen and all the other fleshpots. When I got back to the reserve fleet in Portsmouth I volunteered to play the bugle for 'Colours' [bugle call] in the morning and then volunteered to play 'Colours' in the evening, and they were so excited, they gave me the Admiral's sea cabin in the bridge. I had a shower, I had a bed, I had a bedside light and I had a radio. I had everything – just for playing 'Colours'!

From the navy, John went up to Oxford, taking his trumpet with him. Between tutorials he could be found playing in the University Cellars Band. Meanwhile, in Magdalen Chapel, a new man had just got his hands on the college organ . . .

Dudley Moore was later interviewed about his scholarship for BBC Radio:

It was deemed a very good way of getting into Oxford or Cambridge, an organ scholarship. You can basically waste away three or four years of your life there. But I was so nervous at the first audition for King's College, Cambridge, I couldn't do anything. So when I went up for the audition at Magdalen . . . I was so convinced that I wouldn't get it that I couldn't have cared less. I played and improvised and what not. I knew I wasn't going to get it . . . and then I got it! I remember playing some jazz in Magdalen College Chapel with the doors closed and playing postludes on popular songs, making them sound very grand!

Moore met John Bassett on a production of Thomas Middleton's horror play *The Changeling*. As well as being a great pianist, Moore revealed his gifts on strings.

Dudley had been asked to do the music for *The Changeling* – directed by the now famous Anthony Page – and also to play a very evil violinist. He had to sidle up and down the stairs playing 'evilly', looking like a spider and playing squeaky bits on the violin. Dudley with his smaller stature and gammy leg was thundering up and down the stairs being as menacing as he could, which if you knew him, was not very menacing. To follow me, footling about [on the trumpet], just shows what creative musicality he had, in that he said, 'Play anything with long slow notes and moodiness and I'll follow you upstairs,' because of course he had to go up two flights of stairs to be in the organ loft. At the end of the production he welcomed me to his rooms in Magdalen, where we spent the entire afternoon listening to Erroll Garner records.

The pair shared a passion for the American jazz pianist.

When Dudley and I used to go to Erroll Garner's concerts we both used to have orgasms. Everyone who loves Garner knows what's coming – out of the rubato [not fixed to a tempo], when it comes to two bars beyond what you think he's going to do [go into solid time], he's suddenly going to go 'kerchung!' with his left hand [the beginning of solid 4/4 time] and then it's going to be absolutely metronomic. So Dudley and I would sit in the Festival Hall or wherever holding ourselves in the seats, and the moment that his left hand would hit, we'd sort of go, 'Ooohhh!' It was absolutely wonderful, I can't tell you.

Erroll Garner famously used to sit on the Chicago telephone directory during concerts so that he could reach the keys. He and Moore had much in common: great, inspiring technique and individuality nestled discreetly behind a privet hedge of immense charm, along with the need for a slightly higher chair.

People talk about Dudley, when he was at Oxford, being worried about coming from Dagenham and about being small. I never saw him show the faintest worry about Dagenham, and all that because he was so sure – without being bossy or big-headed – of his talent. He was so sure of his ability. It is true that the organ scholar before Dudley was six foot four and Dudley took over his scholar's gown, and my mother took it up by two foot so that he could walk in it. But, you know, he walked tall, Dudley did, with his ability.

Soon Moore was playing in John Bassett's band the Bassett Hounds. As a jazz pianist he was already outstanding and attracting attention, but his comedic talent was also coming to the fore, as John Bassett remembers.

When you play a stunning solo you get an enormous round

of applause. I don't need to tell you that Dudley played stunning solos, so it wasn't long before the entire audience was roaring its approval for what he was playing. And, warming to that applause as any performer does, it wasn't long again before he got off the chair and started doodling about, being silly and joking, and I think that gave him the confidence to do performances.

He was busking in both cases [as a pianist and as a comic], picking up on the audience musically, and humorously and verbally as well.

It wasn't long before Moore was applying his encyclopaedic knowledge of composition, using it to reconstruct well-known ditties in the arch styles of great composers – music-hall favourites such as 'Daisy, Daisy', 'My Old Man' or 'Doing the Lambeth Walk' à la Chopin, for example – and showing breathtaking skill in comically adapting the operatic style of Benjamin Britten and his distinctive tenor Peter Pears to children's nursery rhymes.

He used to do 'Little Bo Peep' in various styles, of which Benjamin Britten was the most vicious. He was working on those all the time. But I do have one special memory. He played at our drummer's sister's wedding. As they went to sign the wedding register and all that, he played 'Can't Help Loving that Man of Mine' as a Bach chorale. He knew every single musical reference. He could take the mickey out of every infantile tune that he could find.

Dudley's talent was prodigious, but because he was really quite a shy person and a very gentle person and an extremely warm person, it only came upon you ever so gradually, really. I can't remember being bowled over and knocked out with it; it just seemed to be there. Looking back on it is the astonishing part.

After Oxford, the pair went to find work as professional musicians in London's thriving big-band scene.

Dudley got picked up by [dance bandleader] Vic Lewis to play with him, and was a brilliant imitator of Vic. They were both quite small men. There was a lot of musical mutiny in Vic Lewis's ranks and he kept on saying, 'I've had it up to here . . . I've had it up to here, Dudley,' and, of course, 'up to here' was a foot above his head!

The Bassett Hounds continued as a mainstream jazz big band, playing debutante soirées, posh parties and Soho nightclubs. The highlight of this period for John was recording the Bassett Hounds' first album. The band's vibraphonist and Bonzo Dog Doo-Dah Band regular Peter Shade recalls the experience.

The energy that's generated between Dudley and myself, I've never found that with anybody else. The excitement that we generated together was a question of each one listening to the other and then just building on it. The musical rapport was great.

British tenor saxophonist Duncan Lamont was also a band member, and recalls Moore's comedy notepad.

Dudley was always writing things. He always had a notepad. He was probably doing scripts or gags or whatever. In those days that was completely unknown because he was just a piano player.

John tried to use some of the guile he'd developed to protect his embouchure while marching across the navy dockyards to speed up Moore's production of musical arrangements for the Bassett Hounds, which he always seemed to complete with only minutes to spare.

I had to tell him that we'd been commissioned to do it; I had to lie to him that the recording session was a fortnight ahead. He found out just by chance from one of the other musicians that it was actually a fortnight later than he thought. He can only work up to the minute, if you know what I mean, and he finally turned up at the recording studios at ten o'clock the night before the session and spent the night in the studio with three copyists writing out his orchestrations, and by five o'clock in the morning he'd done five orchestrations. I mean, he was totally chaotic in that sense. I'm sure he would take on a commission, I'm sure he would mean to do it well, I'm sure he would do it well; but he would only do it twenty minutes before it was needed.

In addition to walking his Bassett Hounds, John moonlighted as the assistant artistic director of the Edinburgh Festival. Dudley Moore takes up the story from an interview he gave on an American cable network.

> A friend of mine, John Bassett, was working for the Edinburgh festival. Robert Ponsonby was the director and either he or John, my friend, thought of the idea of having a late-night revue at the festival, using university players.

Passing through John Bassett's office in the early part of 1960 were fellow Oxonian Alan Bennett, Jonathan Miller, who had been at Cambridge, and Moore, who was still at the piano. Ponsonby suggested that all three should meet up-and-coming writer Peter Cook, who had penned a successful revue – *Pieces of Eight* – in the West End for *Carry On* star Kenneth Williams. This legendary meeting has now become the most historic bit of matchmaking since the Three Musketeers, as John recalls.

We met in an Italian restaurant opposite Warren Street tube.

I think there ought to be a blue plaque on it. All four met and they were all very, very wary of saying anything funny in case the others didn't laugh at it. Of course the three of them apart from Dudley were thinking of witty, perceptive, incisive, intellectual jokes. Dudley broke the entire atmosphere into hysterics by doing a sort of Groucho Marx walk. The restaurant had double doors into the kitchen. You went in through one with dirty crockery and you came out through another. The waitresses were very pretty and Italian, and Dudley does his Groucho Marx walk behind one who's got dark hair, with plates full of rubbish, and immediately comes out with a blonde with full plates, as if he's changed the girl behind the doors or whatever, but it absolutely broke the atmosphere for the four because we realised that we all laughed at basic practical jokes as well as more intellectual ones. I'm convinced without that the other three would have been singularly more guarded and the atmosphere possibly a little more frigid.

My feeling about that little bit of cabaret was that Dudley was being Dudley. I do think that secretly he may have felt he wasn't verbally as adept as them, but one must remember his practicality.

The result of this foursome coming together was the groundbreaking show *Beyond the Fringe*, the thunderclap that started the satire boom of the sixties. While going on to successful runs in the West End and Broadway, the very first show at the Lyceum in Edinburgh in August 1960 had a nervous start.

In those days you weren't allowed to have the curtain up, and you certainly weren't allowed to have *any* dialogue, until 'God Save the Queen' had been played, so the sketch concerned three very English people who were astounded at the patriotism of the Russian visitor who kept on coming in and playing 'God Save the Queen'. Dudley was the one doing that. Now, we'd been given a dressing room four flights up, so there were three of them murmuring onstage to each other, because they weren't allowed to say words, and we wondered where Dudley was. Very faintly we heard the 'be-dumpfshhh' of a lavatory. He'd been having a pee on the fourth floor, and we knew he'd come down those four floors very slowly and they were going to have to continue murmuring till he got there. He came down whistling without a care in the world until he got into the wings and saw they'd been there for about four minutes!

John's skills as an impresario were obvious and *Beyond the Fringe* was a hit show; a massive hit. But in the feeding frenzy that followed deals were done to transfer it to the West End which left John Bassett out in the cold.

This is where a little bitterness creeps in. While I was up in Edinburgh, Peter Cook's agent Donald Langdon organised the whole West End business and cut me out. What he got me was eighty pounds for four weeks' work if I would do the publicity for the show. I'll always be grateful to co-producer Willy Donaldson, who voluntarily gave me one per cent of his money because he felt I'd been hard done by. It should have been two and a half per cent, but I shouldn't grumble or grouse.

Caryl Brahms [frequent collaborator of Ned Sherrin] christened me the father of English satire. That's overdoing it by far. I like to think of myself as a midwife.

It's certainly more comical to be the midwife of English satire, but the being the midwife is not the same as being the child and the show born of this four-way collaboration quickly became a meteoric success. John soon found his skills were no longer required.

It's true that the show went off without me, but one must remember that one is only a facilitator, like an agent, and it would be hard to think of how they could have lugged me in.

In spite of his being surgically removed from the West End version of *Beyond the Fringe*, John's musical friendship with Moore blossomed. Moore now found himself in the superheated steam of success. After every performance of *Beyond the Fringe* he would spend all night playing jazz at Peter Cook's Soho nightclub, the Establishment.

Dudley was immensely attractive to women. I was astounded to see, sitting on the small stage under the grand piano, three or four girls swept up with Dudley and waiting to see which one he would take home. Can't tell you how jealous I was.

Peter Shade recalls Moore's spontaneity.

I remember at the Establishment once a woman came up and was tapping the piano. She wanted to attract Dudley's attention and she said, 'I say, piano! Piano! You haven't played a waltz all evening!' and he leapt off the stage holding her in his arms going, 'La, la-la, la, la, la, la, la, la' [the tune to 'Tenderly'], dancing a waltz with her. It was so funny. She was totally taken aback.

Duncan Lamont remembers seeing the breakneck speed of Moore's hectic life at this time.

At the time I thought the pace was killing because he never stopped. He was working, he was entertaining, he was playing, he was romancing . . . he was partying . . . [*Laughs*]

John was a part of the action too, but could tell that his friend was moving into different circles.

Dudley was part of me and apart from me. He went off with Peter [Cook], and of course I came down to see *Beyond the Fringe* just about every night and every weekend and I was a part of it, but they were already leading off and you've got the wonderful series they did on the BBC [*Not Only . . . But Also . . .*] and all that. I was a very happy viewer of that and I was happy talking to Dudley about it, but it's not me. He'd moved on by then, you know.

With the transfer of Beyond the Fringe to Broadway, Moore's path to fame was assured. Life in New York, while opulent, retained a distinctive 'studenty' feel, as John recalls.

Dudley had rented a flat from the star of *Kiss Me, Kate*. She had an artistic leaning, but only paint by numbers; so there was *The Blue Boy* paint by numbers, the *Mona Lisa* paint by numbers – not repro but paint by numbers all over the flat. Dudley had originally rented it for himself and his hoped-for girlfriend, Celia Hammond. Eventually, he said I could stay as I had nowhere to go. He and I slept in two gargantuan double beds, and if you've ever seen Dudley in an emperor-size bed, he gets lost. There we were, in these gargantuan beds watching telly, and I was beginning to worry because Celia was due to arrive and I knew he'd want to get me out. So he started dropping a hint or two.

Eventually he agreed I could stay in the double emperor-size bedroom and he would move with Celia into the other single emperor-sized bedroom, but we would have had to make sure there was no sound from one to the other. So Dudley went into the room he was going to share with Celia and made what he thought were female orgasmic noises, while I stayed in the main room to see if I could hear any squeak whatsoever. Now (a) that was ludicrous, and (b) it should have been the other way round. Dudley should have reassured himself that he couldn't hear orgasmic noises by staying in the main bedroom while I made them. However, I said I hadn't heard a dicky bird.

Dudley Moore went on to have considerable success in America with a string of films, starting with the brilliant and much overlooked *Bedazzled* (1967) with Peter Cook. He scored the soundtrack to this and others. But it was in the late-seventies that he landed his massive Hollywood hit film *10*, co-starring Bo Derek. He had another movie hit with *Arthur* in 1981.

Meanwhile, back in Britain, John Bassett trained as a producer at Granada TV, worked with Ned Sherrin on the satirical TV show *That Was the Week That Was* and, while working at the theatrical agents Curtis Brown, discovered Eric Chappell's timeless sitcom *Rising Damp*, originally titled *The Banana Box*.

John frequently visited Moore in Los Angeles and they maintained close contact. In 1999 Moore was diagnosed with progressive supranuclear palsy, a rare brain disorder. He died in 2002.

There's a sadness at the end of Dudley's life. Not only that he died young, but that Dudley lost the use of his hands first. To realise you can never again play to your standard is just horrific. The phone calls to me came to an end. I wrote to him a lot and didn't expect letters back. Sadly, and it may have been his wish – I don't know – but the very kind family he was with wouldn't allow anyone, repeat *anyone*, to go and see him. I sent him some photos, but he may not want to have been reminded of the fun of long ago while *in extremis*.

Former Bassett Hound saxophonist Duncan Lamont.

I was thinking about Dudley the other day and I really miss

him around. I never saw Dudley after he became successful in movies but I feel there was a contact. A wonderful guy and a wonderful musician.

Bassett Hounds vibraphonist Peter Shade.

Whatever 'it' is, he had 'it' in bucketfuls. And it's a shame that later on in life that wasn't developed more because he went more into film and other things, when in actual fact his musicality was the thing and communicated with everyone. A fabulous character.

In an interview with the BBC's *In Town Tonight* from 1960, Moore said . . .

Being a composer or playing the piano is really the same as being a comedian; you're playing with emotions, you're expressing emotions, you're playing with time. If you play the piano you have to time your playing and if you're being a comedian you have to time your laughs.

For John, the greatest sadness was that circumstances prevented him from seeing more of his friend.

Since I didn't see Dud's illness, every recollection I have of him is of enormous good humour and fun and laughs and hysteria and competitions in seduction.

Dudley Moore left an incredible, peerless legacy that included landmark comedy, original compositions, film scores, ballets and operas and an astonishing musicianship. All of it packaged in the kind of humility rarely seen in world-class, gifted performers.
John Bassett is in no doubt about Moore's human qualities.

Dudley is just total larking. He always lifted every meeting he was a part of, he lifted it up and made it memorable;

musically, humorously, intelligently, warmly, humanely. He was just a great guy.

My recollections of dear old Duddles are so happy and so varied, so interesting, so warm and so everything that it reminded me of that wonderful line of Joe Gargery's in *Great Expectations* saying, 'What larks eh, Pip? What larks!'

12

I Was Morrissey's Drummer

I said, 'That's interesting – you've got a gold disc of *Viva Hate*. How have you got that?' And Andrew said something like, 'Yes, well, you know, when one's drummed for Morrissey one wants to remember it.'

Mark Kermode

I'm Andrew McGibbon, though some of you may know me as Andrew Paresi.

I played drums on nine of Morrissey's top-twenty UK singles between 1987 and 1991: 'Suedehead', 'Every Day Is Like Sunday', 'Ouija Board, Ouija Board', 'Piccadilly Palare', 'November Spawned a Monster', 'Our Frank', 'Sing Your Life', 'Pregnant for the Last Time' and 'My Love Life'. I also played on his albums *Viva Hate*, *Bona Drag* and *Kill Uncle*, and I'd have played on more albums if I hadn't suddenly had to take up a post as deputy consul general in Malawi. (OK, that last bit isn't true.)

Of course, I continue to play the drums today, and the chances are you've heard me many times without realising it, but drumming for Morrissey in the eighties took me to a universe where feeling, emotion and freedom to create were all that mattered. Once I'd been there as a drummer in the context of rockular music, I felt that this was probably going to be the greatest experience of my musical career. Nothing was ever going to come close or be worth the effort of trying to achieve. As it happened, this sudden insight neatly coincided with a period of enforced unemployment, thus relieving me of making any effort whatsoever.

Drummers all appear to come from a similar tribe. It is one devoted to intense competition, anxiety about one's own talents, self-aggrandisement, flash, show-off charisma and, most of all, ineffable self-indulgence. Drummers need to construct a tubular stockade from what appear to be angular mounted coffee tables and heavy bronze lampshades. Once it's built, they climb inside and hide there like funnel-web spiders, ready to leap out during a drum fill. Often they are the strongest personalities in any group. A drummer's mutually exclusive desires to be onstage and loved by the crowds while hidden behind a scaffold of metal and wood results in a kind of bi-polar, backbeating entity inhabiting a polyrhythmical world that no one cares about but everybody pretends to understand and even find, er, sensitive and emotional. (One employer described my drumming as nuggets of rhythmic gold wrapped up in a fondant toffee and chocolate coating. She wasn't bad herself, as it goes.)

In the end it comes down to this: 'Love me, love me, but leave me alone behind the latticework of my solitary prison . . . Look at me go; I'm a genius . . . Stop looking at me; I'm rubbish . . . You love me, I hate you; I love you, I hate myself . . . What a pretentious dick I must look like sitting at this Ikea-styled elaborate solo gym-workout machine behind these bastards who are going to fire me afterwards anyway . . .'

Then the band starts playing . . .

If the average drummer was a viable tunesmith – like, say, Levon Helm of the Band, who could sing beautifully behind his kit – many of these anxieties would be expunged by the joyful expressions on the faces in the front row. But drummers don't usually see the crowds or the faces and don't play sweet tunes on a keyboardy thing or a guitar, so drumming is a uniquely physical, achromatic, rhythmic activity.

I don't think I've ever come across a more sorry bunch of wankers in my life.

You'd think that being able to tap into the beautiful wells of the universal rhythm that is in everything would make them all only too happy to be there – the bodhisattvas of beat. Sorry. Not true.

Take it from me, only a gifted few are like that. The rest are a bunch of tossers. If rhythm is a vast open space as far as the inner eye can see, drummers are the little minds living in the tiny thatched cottage in the only valley behind the only tree.

When you're hidden from view there's really no point in complaining about not being seen. Therein lies the drummer's paradox. They're the suburbanites of rock music, hiding outside the conurbations but laying down a beat dressed as Batman at a Spider-Man party. In the end they have to face their demons and become entertainers, because they're not tunesmiths or singers – they're just the physical movement at the back of the stage.

Whenever I've caught sight of myself drumming on TV, I'm often struck by the fact that my intense expression – sweating, mouth open, thrusting waist and torso movements emanating from bouncing hips – suggests I'm in a metal-themed gonzo porn movie with the bottom half of the screen blanked out by the forest of wood and steel. It's not a pretty sight.

Only when people like Keith Moon (headcase), Ringo Starr (funster), Charlie Watts (coolest) or Mick Fleetwood (tallest) play with great character and style does drumming start looking like a respectable artistic operation.

This is what I struggled with during the early part of my career: I wanted to look as great as I knew I played. I've got the formula right now, and if you follow me into this brightly lit soundproofed room, I'll show you what I mean. (Ignore the cameraman.)

Here's what some very important people in the music industry think about drummers. British national treasure Suggs, of Madness:

They're the least intelligent of the group, obviously, because they bash their brains out and they like to spend hours and hours going boom-boom-boom-boom, individually, on the drums before the rest of the band arrive, before the rest of the band are even in the same country . . . and they get on better with the road crew because they're on the same intellectual level.

Here's Coldplay's producer Danton Supple:

I guess they're a bit like lab rats in lots of ways. Give them some input and record the results.

I asked legendary record producer Clive Langer the ultimate question: What do you think of drummers?

[*Silence*]

You've nothing to say?

[*Shakes head*]

OK.

I feel very privileged to have found rhythm. The trouble is that it's addictive and requires a daily fix. If I don't play the drums I start clicking my teeth together like a fitful snoozing bull mastiff dreaming of ripping the lungs out of a toy poodle. Then I start making demented rhythms with my mouth, which make me sound like a mad simpleton and will one day get me sectioned. I'm passionate about drumming and I can't help it. Rhythm is the Uniter. Groove is King. Once you understand these things you have found a personal religious conviction that will forever isolate you from normal people – a jester with a small beard who does stick tricks and drum rudiments for the King and Queen in court while tailoring bespoke rhythms for the ladies-in-waiting.

But enough about drumming. More about me.

To really understand what motivated me to play the drums, we have to go right back, almost to the beginning. I picked up my first pair of drumsticks at the tender age of . . . sixteen. I practised and practised and practised to make up the time I'd lost, until I was red in the face.

But Destiny's elevator rose very slowly, and actually jammed at one point. I worked in rundown bars, seedy shopping malls and a big hotel near London airport, and it was in exactly this place late one evening – New Year's Eve, to be precise – when a man approached me and asked me to come up to his bedroom and play bongos while he cavorted with a call girl before returning to his wives in the Middle East.

Seeing an opportunity to advance my percussion skills, I jumped at the two fifty-pound notes he was dangling, kept my acetate leopardskin shirt and safari suit firmly on and agreed to see in the New Year as part of the evening's entertainment. When the hotel manager used a master key to enter the room after receiving complaints from other hotel guests whose call girls were being put off by the racket, I was fired and had my bongos punctured to prevent any further rhythmic revelry.

Far worse, though, I had lost my way as a drummer. What was I doing playing standards in hotel lobbies and dressing like a warm-up act for Siegfried and Roy? What was wrong with me? Where was my moral compass, my artistic rectitude? Why, it was here all along in the pockets of my safari suit . . . Two fifty-pound notes. If a bright, educated guy was stupid enough to think this was a good living, then he must have been a drummer. There is simply no other explanation.

Having lost my regular gig at the hotel, I was thrown onto the pointy shards of uncertainty. Homeless for six months, I slept on prostitutes' floors, sometimes even on prostitutes, often being mistaken for a client who hadn't paid.

Then, in the mid-eighties, it all changed. In this sparkling, sexy decade everything was shiny, tight and backcombed and people were wearing big spectacles, rainbow T-shirts and leg-warmers! Back then, sartorial dullness was a crime on a parallel with animal buggery. I did my best, but frankly I didn't really cut it. I wore bright trousers, wanky shoes and ridiculously baggy jumpers that made me look like one of Gyles Brandreth's wig pimps.

At this time pop music had been showing its deep and meaningless side. There were great pop bands knocking about, breakthrough studio production techniques, pioneers like Trevor Horn producing sweet-sounding pop bands like Dollar, and Radio 1 was pumping out superb-sounding music on a crunched-up bandwidth that compressed everything to make it sound even poppier. The Human League, ABC, Spandau Ballet, Duran Duran, Japan and, best and most intriguing of all, Adam and the Ants. All these groups were injecting colour into a vapid and typically stale British mindset, weary with winters of discontent and state assets being sold off to pay for Mark Thatcher's out-of-date rocket launchers.

But the patina of early-eighties pop started to flake off very soon and when the record companies began to see the rising sales of mid-eighties mammoth bands like Dire Straits, Queen and Genesis, atrophy set in and pop jesters started wearing ponytails and white pixie boots. Some would rather they'd been wearing concrete boots.

Nevertheless, this sad environment was my musical nest and I was busy warming a clutch of soulless ambitions, conning myself into thinking I was only a few years away from becoming a successful muso with permed hair, fake tan, Afghan hound, a house in Crystal Palace and an ex-backing-singer wife. But something profound was about to happen to me.

There were two key British obsessions in the eighties: one was certain annihilation by a nuclear weapon, the other was

Bucks Fizz. I was lucky enough to drum on the first and probably only song ever to be recorded by Bucks Fizz about nuclear war. Called 'I Used to Love the Radio', it is a lament to how wonderful it was to hear the radio in the days before nuclear annihilation. Protect and survive meets porn pop. Looking back now it's hard to unite these disparate elements. But as I recall the shotglass, red-rimmed hopelessness of the eighties, the Buck and Fizz of the ... er ... yes, it didn't make sense then, either.

I drummed on another song of theirs, 'Love in a World Gone Mad', with lyrics penned by Pete Sinfield, the man who wrote the words to King Crimson's 'In the Court of the Crimson King'. It was the follow-up single to Bucks Fizz's triumphant return to form with 'Mamba Seyra (New Beginning)', after the near-fatal coach crash that interrupted their early career.

Finally, I began to feel I was getting my feet in the door.

I'd also played on a number-one single by Jim Diamond, 'I Should Have Known Better' from 1984. That is, I'd mimed the drumming of Badfinger's Simon Kirke on ITV's *Razzamatazz*, but my Bucks Fizz studio dates now made me feel like part of the in-crowd of sessioneers. This idyll was a false one, though.

Suggs remembers the mid-eighties undertow: an obsession with death by mutually assured destruction.

We got very involved in CND and I remember going round Trafalgar Square, and Michael Heseltine had a load of loudspeakers out of his apartment playing military marching music. He was shouting out of a loudhailer, going, 'This is real marching music, you hear me, you long-haired yobbos . . .' What a disorientating sight that was . . . for him.

But back in the thick dark bush of popular music, things were stirring. Indie-student rock fans were beginning to feel left out of the coke-nosed, Concorde-flying, Live Aid helicopter cock-rockracy that was ruling the radio. But students have a habit of finding things that annoy grown-ups, especially big fat plutocrat-shaped ones to whom Radio I was in thrall. There was some political anarchist rock popping up on John Peel's late-night radar, but nothing that seemed to offer anything funny or entertaining amidst the earnestness of pop-music subversion during the early eighties.

Then, in May 1983, the Smiths arrived.

Like a three-way shotgun marriage between Ena Sharples, Oscar Wilde and Victoria Wood, the Smiths managed to be sexy, literate, funny, fey and waspish, as well as being one of the greatest pop bands ever. A phenomenon which is likely to appear only once in a generation and be referenced for as long as it is possible to keep music listenable for future generations. Which may be ten to twenty minutes if you believe the lyrics to 'I Used to Love the Radio'.

Mark Kermode is a rabid Smiths fan, a rockabilly bass player and a film critic. He understood where Morrissey was coming from.

If you found Morrissey funny then the Smiths were a really great band, and the people who hated the Smiths and hated Morrissey later on never found any of that stuff funny. I mean, I was always really charmed by anyone writing songs about, you know, 'everything's awful, my life's terrible, no one loves me . . . ohhh . . . I woke up this morning and I was still here and I was still me and you're not here and you threw me out of bed . . .', because to me that's really funny, but equally I understand people who listen to that and go, 'Shut up, you whingeing ninny.'

Suggs remembers goin' doon pit with the Smiths. Pop was hard in those days. All you had was a Davy lamp to light a snout with, and a canary for company.

My first contact with Morrissey was on *Top of the Pops*, which is always a strange environment, and I do remember we were performing 'Night Boat to Cairo' in pith helmets and khaki shorts, and on the other stage was Morrissey singing 'Heaven Knows I'm Miserable Now', and Dexy's Midnight Runners were performing, so I suddenly had this disorientating feeling of being a children's entertainer at a very serious party, you know, that I was being ignored at.

Meanwhile, as this non-daytime-radio pop group the Smiths was swallowing up everyone's attention, I tried to capitalise career-wise on all the excellent drumming and sessions I'd done ... by working for two years as a medical assistant in the Edenham Rest Home in Westbourne Grove, which has now been pulled down to make way for younger people.

Of course I still played – well, I was also a musician, for heaven's sake. In fact, I was the only brown-eyed member of a blue-eyed soul band signed to CBS, now Sony, whose first single was being mixed by Smiths' producer Stephen Street.*

I remember working on the track and being very impressed with the drumming on it . . .

In the late summer of 1987 the Smiths split up after an argument about what the regulation size of a peach cobbler should be or something. That September, Stephen asked me to play drums on some songs he had written with Morrissey after the split. These songs would be part of the sessions for Morrissey's first solo album, *Viva Hate*.

Stephen Street recalls the events leading up to my first encounter with Morrissey.

---

* The band was called A Pair of Blue Eyes, as in the short story by Thomas Hardy. Muff Winwood, then head of A&R at CBS, allegedly called us 'the thinking man's Curiosity Killed the Cat'.

At the end of the summer of 1987, after the Smiths had broken up, I had sent off this cassette to Morrissey with some ideas I thought could be used for B-sides to forthcoming Smiths singles, and he sent me a postcard back saying, 'I want to make an album.' So I met him and I said, 'What do we do now?' and he said, 'Have you got any idea who we could work with?' I said, 'Well, I've got this drummer in mind who could do a really fine job on the record. Would you like me to arrange a meeting?'

I still wasn't sure why I'd been picked from the thousands who were never auditioned.

One thing was certain: I'd been chosen for my drumming, not my appearance, as I dressed like a failed *Blue Peter* presenter. So I was tidied up and presented to Morrissey at Stephen Street's flat. This dazzlingly symmetrical charmster, sporting tumescent quiff and limpid NHS specs, was the most beautiful creature I'd ever seen.

Stephen Street was wrestling with the correct combination of studio personnel.

It was very hard to think of, you know, the right kind of people to put in the studio with Morrissey because he's very particular – if he doesn't like you, he'll completely blank you. So it was very important I chose the people carefully to come and help me make the first record.

And so I'd become Morrissey's drummer. Of course, saying 'I Was Morrissey's Drummer' is a little bit like saying 'I Was Cary Grant's Agent', or 'I Was Jack Ruby's Tailor', or 'I Was Robin Cook's Hair Colourist'. The truth is you're simply travelling with fame and putting its cat out at night. My brush with renown came as a surprise to some people – Mark Kermode, for one.

One day I was round at Andrew's place doing something for a comedy show he was making and I noticed there were gold discs on the wall and I said, 'That's interesting – you've got a gold disc of *Viva Hate*. How have you got that?' And Andrew said something like, 'Yes, well, you know, when one's drummed for Morrissey one wants to remember it.' And I laughed and he said, 'I have drummed for Morrissey.' I said, 'No, you haven't!' He said, 'Yes, I have . . . I Was Morrissey's Drummer.' This seemed like somebody saying to me, 'I was the fifth member of the Beatles' – it seemed like such an insane thing to have been. And then of course I looked around and realised that the other things in the studio were a drum kit, which should have been a dead giveaway, and a bunch of gold discs that were indeed the Morrissey solo albums.

But I was just a hired hand, there to channel the spirits of rhythm into the pools of tune and bond them into a seamless mesh of hum-hash. My compadres on this journey were Durutti Column guitarist Vini Reilly and bass player and producer Stephen Street, who wrote the music. Working out which parts of the music were choruses and which parts were verses was rather difficult, until Morrissey sang a guide or final vocal on the recording – assuming we had done it right, as Stephen Street recalls.

I would play the rough demos of a song to Vini and Andrew, give Vini the chords, go downstairs [the control room was upstairs, with the live area below] and play bass, with Andrew on the drums, and then Morrissey would put his vocal on and, ahhh . . . now we know what's going to happen on it.

When 'Suedehead', the first single off the album, was released it had what is known in radiospeak as 'heavy rotation' on the nation's favourite, Radio 1. The station had rarely played any Smiths tracks on its daytime shows, yet in the three weeks before it was available in the shops 'Suedehead' was being played four, sometimes five times a day on Radio 1 alone. This was the first time in nine years of struggling with an unpredictable career that I was now hearing my drumming on the radio, and it was glorious. It was like nothing else I'd ever experienced. It wasn't my record in the sense that I was the artist, but the way I'd played on it – very loud and hard (remember, this is pre-Nirvana) – made the drums stand out on the recording and the compressors used on Radio 1 made it sound even more strident and bouncy.

It was amazing to hear it and take in what all the presenters were saying after it was played. This was a significant event and my snare, hi-hat and bass drum were all over it! It was pure joy.

Stephen Street would go on to produce many hit records for Blur and the Kaiser Chiefs, amongst others. He remembers the building of 'Suedehead'.

The top line is a Vini Reilly riff. It could have been suggested by the opening drum fill, the dat, dat, dat, dah . . . thing; I don't know, because it picks up on the same beat in the bar. The reason I love 'Suedehead' so much is that it was the first one we'd cut in the studio where I felt the contributions from both Vini and Andrew were spot on, and it made that track come alive.

The next single released was 'Every Day Is Like Sunday'. Like 'Suedehead', it made it into the top ten and is regarded by many who know about these things as a classic English pop single. It is certainly the most lyrically stimulating – nuclear bomb explodes over Skegness as Morrissey is writing a postcard about how dull it is. Quite brilliant. Mark Kermode agrees.

'Every Day Is Like Sunday' is a classic Morrissey record, again because it's Morrissey doing that classic, drop an atom bomb on this seaside town, wet sand . . . and it's got that big, romping apocalyptic feel to it, and it's a classic post-Smiths Morrissey pop song – it's big, it's aware of its own ridiculousness. It's ironic because 'Every Day Is Like Sunday' is supposed to be an upbeat thing, but in fact it's because everything is silent and grey, everything is awful, no one still loves me and everything is terrible.

The song reflects an earlier age of seaside towns, perhaps during the mid-sixties, when everyone was jetting off to the Costa del Sol and the English seaside was deserted and left to rot. Sunday trading had only just taken off when it was released and the day of rest was a far cry from the bumper-to-bumper shopping fest it has since become. Mark Kermode is waving his arms . . .

Again with 'Suedehead' and 'Every Day Is Like Sunday', they are classic air-drumming tracks and it starts . . . bum, bum, bum . . . and then you start WAVING YOUR ARMS AROUND . . . and 'Suedehead', because it's got that backwards guitar bit at the beginning, then DA DA DA DUM at the beginning . . . I have air-drummed to those songs on several occasions.

The album *Viva Hate* went straight to number one in the UK charts in March 1987. It was released on my birthday. Alongside its two flagship singles, it contained other songs which had been a joy to play the drums on. Stephen Street explains what he and Morrissey were looking for.

'Late Night, Maudlin Street' came out of this second batch of songs. The type of drumming on that song, to work, would have to be more American, kind of jazzy rather than Britpop drumming. It was perfect.

In fact, Morrissey and Stephen had been listening to Joni Mitchell's *The Hissing of Summer Lawns* and a track off Rickie Lee Jones's eponymous solo album called 'Last Chance Texaco'. In 'Late Night, Maudlin Street' Stephen and Morrissey wanted the drumming to start coming in around the point in the song where life for its subject is changing dramatically.

Here's the section described as a drummer might understand it . . .

When the instrumental verse comes in the drummer plays a very loose double-time samba with a variety of fills and cross-rhythms backed up with eights [quavers] pedalled on the hi-hat, and very occasionally the bass drum, accenting cymbals and firing the occasional demisemiquaver. He uses a lot of five-stroke rolls, odd accents and grace notes with the fills standing out in an angular way so as to underscore the emotions in the song.

The illustration shows what the first part of it looks like on manuscript as a drummer might read it.

Late Night, Maudlin Street (Morrissey/Street. From the CD "Viva Hate" 1988 Parlophone/EMI)

Stephen Street recalls other key non-drumming events and excursions during the recording of *Viva Hate* at the Wool Hall, a residential studio in Somerset owned by Tears for Fears.

When we were making that first album, I can remember doing things like playing charades in the cottage [the Wool Hall had a separate cottage for musicians to sleep and eat in] and you never saw him [Morrissey] playing charades with the Smiths; you know, they'd be getting absolutely bollocked somewhere and he'd be in bed . . . But it was very English, and I think he enjoyed it. The Wool Hall and the recordings gave him a definite rock to cling to in those post-Smiths, traumatic months he was going through.

The launch party for *Viva Hate* took place in a seedy nightclub in Bath. Stephen Street forced me to wear his denim jacket and put the rest of my outfit in a lime bath, as he recalls.

Well, I think Morrissey sort of said something like, 'I wouldn't be seen dead with Andrew looking like that. If he's coming out with us tonight he's going to have to look a little sharper than that.' He didn't say it as such but you could just tell by the look, you know. [*Laughs*] So I said, 'Andrew, have you thought about wearing this jacket?'

Launch parties are supposed to be roaring, glamorous affairs, packed to the point of no breathable oxygen; intense, overwhelming and noisy, with photographers taking millions of pictures of you, even though you are a nobody. But the launch party for *Viva Hate* was so quiet that many punters thought the club was closed for redecoration.

Yet to know that I had the drumming chair for an entire album and the freedom to experiment with expressive and different styles was a double joy. I felt unassailable and relieved. There would be no muscled fuckstick barging his way onto my throne and cracking jokes that everyone in the band laughed at. I knew that no other drummer could make me redundant. Only Morrissey could do that.

And he did.

Stephen Street offers an explanation:

Morrissey wrote to me a couple of months later and said, 'I want to do another session. I've chosen these tracks you've sent me, I'd like to work on those . . . however, I would like to work with Mike [Joyce] and Andy [Rourke], the original Smiths rhythm section. Have you any problem with that?'

I bummed around a bit again, for about eighteen months. In that time I came close to losing my flat. In the end I had no choice but to sell my beloved drum kit to pay the mortgage.

The next day I was hired to play with Morrissey again.

I happened to be in a studio with Kevin Armstrong, a guitarist who had often played for David Bowie, when a call came in from producer Clive Langer asking Kevin to play on some new songs he was recording with Morrissey. Kevin recommended me to Clive, Clive then spoke to Morrissey and I was back in as Morrissey's drummer.

This time I took control of the situation. I made sure that my position was secure by taking action to ensure I was in complete charge. The new producers of this project, Clive Langer and Alan Winstanley, of Madness and Dexy's Midnight Runners fame, were serious operators and I didn't want to give the impression I wasn't a professional . . .

I didn't want to, but I did anyway, turning up for the session with a drum kit that would have shamed a primary-school music department. In spite of this woeful professional lapse on my part I was allowed to stay. The recording, which began with the single 'Ouija Board, Ouija Board' and continued with 'Yes, I Am Blind' and 'The Girl Least Likely To', would go on to become part of *Bona Drag*, the *Mary Celeste* of Morrissey's solo records.

I had a rather jolly time at Langer and Winstanley's comfortable and capacious studio, Hook End Manor near Reading, once the home of the Cadbury family and Pink Floyd's David Gilmour (though not at the same time). I also made some new friends, such as Andy Rourke, bass player of the Smiths, who recalls the febrile atmosphere at the start of recording.

You'd see Morrissey and expect to see Johnny [Marr] and Mike [Joyce] come in and instead see a room full of strangers . . . so everybody was a little bit nervous and twitchy.

Hook End Manor was quite a place to make recordings. A perfect rock 'n' roll haunt. Def Leppard and Guns N' Roses had been in there a week before, and while they were there it was all-night parties, eager rock chicks and plenty of fornication.

As soon as Morrissey arrived with his band, however, it turned into a Jesuit retreat complete with vegetarian chef deacon, a Catholic priest in the control room at all times and . . . plenty of fornication. Suggs was there too.

I was invited down there by Clive, who was producing the record and said that Morrissey was a fan of Madness and would like to meet me, and that was it, really. We had a rather stilted introduction in a public house, of course, because Mozzer's a big fan of pubs; then we had a punchup and a game of darts, which was nice. No . . . erm . . . he was rather shy, as I am most of the time, but it soon warmed up and the idea was mooted that I might go and sing on a couple of the tracks that had been recorded.

Suggs sang on the uproarious 'Get Off the Stage' and 'Piccadilly Palare', on which he added disturbing and disarming spoken and sung vocal inserts. To this day 'Piccadilly Palare' remains for me a superb recording. Clive Langer gives a definitive insight into working with Morrissey.

> He gave us loads of freedom but without knowledge of what we were doing. We were free to do whatever he wanted, but he didn't define what was happening till he did his vocal and then you weren't allowed to mess with it too much afterwards. So there was a bit of freedom and it was structured, and we wanted to impress Morrissey with what we'd been doing when he came down for his tea, you know.

All great songs come from real experiences. Suggs remembers Morrissey experiencing something for himself which might have inspired one of the tracks on *Bona Drag*.

> I remember going to his room one night when we were at Hook End and I went upstairs and knocked on his door and I could hear this tap, tap, tap and all the lights were off and he was going round the room with a blind stick. Now, what would you put that down to? I don't know.

The B-side to 'Ouija Board, Ouija Board' was 'Yes, I Am Blind'.
'November Spawned a Monster', another single released in April 1990, remains an astonishing piece of work: a powerful song with a terrifying instrumental section, featuring an improvised birthing sequence performed by Canadian singer Mary Margaret O'Hara. Gothic, grotesque and disturbing, it seemed the Radio 1 playlist committee simply didn't have the stomach to air the whole thing, let alone play it at all during the day. Even Nicky Campbell, then presenting a late-night 'music too interesting to be played at any other time'-type show, played the song and faded it out just as the middle section started. It was like being garrotted by a clown. Apart from the insult of fading out what was obviously an overwhelmingly fascinating

recording by Morrissey, it was also some of my best recorded drumming, so I was more than a little pissed off.

Clive Langer wrote the music for 'November'.

Morrissey used to talk about a mood he wanted for a song and I'd go off and have a little go. He would reject some of the tunes I thought were the strongest. That was Morrissey's way. I always gave in to whatever he wanted. And you know, with 'November Spawned a Monster', the part I thought was a chorus he would make into a verse, etc., so he'd change your whole outlook in the course of writing.

Andy Rourke played a superb bass line on the song.

Bass-wise it's one of the ones I'm most proud of.

Clive Langer also felt fulfilled.

'November' is obviously my proudest moment with him.

There was no 'band' as such, just a series of musicians who would arrive, often bringing with them musical ideas that Morrissey might use. I was one of them. I had written the outlines of three songs during this time, one of which came close to having a vocal recorded on it, with the working title of 'Angie'. Kevin Armstrong was another journeyman. At the time he was practising Nichiren Shoshu Buddhism rather too enthusiastically, as Andy Rourke recollects.

I used to sleep in the room next to him and every morning at about six o'clock he used to start chanting and dinging his bells – I wanted to strangle him.

Clive Langer remembers how his routines had to alter for the sake of the project.

You know when you work with Morrissey, he kind of

becomes your wife and so you have to give up other parts of your life, and then you make the decision whether that's worth it or not. For me it was worth it. I felt a lot of love for him but I never depended on anything for him . . . it's a weird love.

Andy Rourke reminisces on the opulent and entertaining evening meals.

The highlight of the day was mealtime. It was like the Last Supper; nobody would eat until he'd started and nobody would attack the wine until he'd tasted it . . .

Well, he was the host, after all. Dinner was also sometimes memorable for very different reasons. Often a musician who'd played that day and showed potential promise for other tracks would stay for dinner, only to have disappeared the next morning – sent packing by the producers under instruction from the host. Morrissey made more people disappear than David Copperfield.

One morning, having had a fitful night's sleep, delirious, hallucinating and haunted by feelings of self-harm, I confronted Morrissey on how wounded I'd been by his decision to use Smiths drummer Mike Joyce on two singles, 'Last of the Famous International Playboys' and 'Interesting Drug', as I felt we had clicked so well during the recording of Viva Hate. Morrissey always rises early for breakfast and, expecting to have the dawn chorus for company, found himself instead being talked to death by a sugar-crazed, back-beater vomiting a fountain of hurt. In the face of my hysterical outburst he was an absolute gentleman; he pointed out gently (though not in these words) that it was his career not mine, and a personal connection was made between us, one that survived beyond the Kill Uncle sessions of 1991.

There were some good reviews for the *Kill Uncle* record-ings, which followed the *Bona Drag* sessions. Mark E. Nevin of Fairground Attraction was retained as principal songwriter, Clive Langer and Alan Winstanley remaining as producers. With Mark Bedford (Bedders of Madness) on bass guitar, there was a common theme to the album – Madness meets Fairground Attraction; English working-class rock.

I sang backing vocals on the second song released from the album, 'Sing Your Life', as did Suggs.

I think 'Sing Your Life' was a lovely song. It was one of those songs where you think, 'Was that written about me?' as you so often do, being egotistical as most of us are in this industry, as the sentiment was that anyone can sing as long as it's in your own voice and you sing about the things you understand, which was something that was very important to me in my own career. I remember we did a vaguely yob-bish chorus, possibly a drink or two, a crowd sequence, and I think it turned out very well.

'Mute Witness' was another outstanding track. Harking back to the style of seventies LA glam band Sparks, it drew the attention of music critic-turned-genius comedy writer David Quantick, who was one of the few journalists to give the album a really good review.

I remember the press officer playing the track to me. It sounded like Sparks or early Roxy Music, and I was excited by that tune because I thought it would be a new direction for Morrissey.

For Clive Langer, *Kill Uncle* was overshadowed by events taking place elsewhere in the pop world.

It was like we'd created a book of poetry with music behind

it for *Kill Uncle*, and I was very proud of that. It was a pity that the Happy Mondays and all that stuff was happening at the same time, because we didn't get a look in. They were on a fashion elevator and we were just making a record.

Having finished drumming on Morrissey's new single 'My Love Life', with backing vocals supplied by Chrissie Hynde, I headed off with Morrissey and the boys in the band to the Camden Working Men's Social Club for an evening of pride and Celtic Hover Skittles. Once inside, surrounded by quiffed and tattooed bopsters, some of whom would go on to become future band members, Morrissey leant back against the wall and said that he was in heaven, that he completely belonged here, that this is where he'd always wanted to be, that these were his people and that this . . . I forget exactly what he said, but from that moment, I knew I was fired.

And not just me. The revolving doors of fortune began to disgorge the quiffless casualties of change. Andy Rourke remembers the sensation that departure was imminent.

At the end of the session I had a feeling that [Morrissey] wasn't going to carry on [with us] and plus . . . I no longer had a rockabilly hairdo.

Clive Langer was also not immune to circumstances.

I was in, I was out, you know . . . that's the way Morrissey works.

And I was out, too, though I did join in the rockabilly drumming fun by turning a kitchen bin upside down and using it as the rhythm basis for another Morrissey single, 'Pregnant for the Last Time', a truly superb song which sounded great and ensured the bin would itself be binned.

After that I took a sabbatical from drumming to concentrate on comedy, writing, producing, directing and performing. I've worked on Radio 1, playing a string of characters on air and writing jokes for the breakfast show, and on Radios 4 and 5. I've also written for comedy shows on BBC1, BBC2 and Channel 4. And, as I said earlier, I still play all the time, although my drumming and humour are not to everyone's taste. Viewers of *Last of the Summer Wine*, for example, probably wish it was me hurtling down the hill in the out-of-control bathtub seen every week on the show.

Luckily, Stephen Street doesn't watch *Last of the Summer Wine*.

I think Andrew's sense of humour really did keep the session flowing, in the sense that if you could keep Morrissey chuckling and have a laugh then that really helps quite a lot. It really does.

Andy Rourke wasn't sure what kind of a drummer he was playing with half the time.

It was like *Michael Bentine's Potty Time* every day; lots of jokes and witty comments coming all the time. He is very good, very solid, pulled some great facial expressions as he whacked the snare like he meant it . . . I'm speaking like he's dead.

And Danton Supple could only watch in horror.

What you do get is a whole host of voices, so when the talkback goes down you never really know who's going to come singing back from the drum kit. Plus there's a certain aesthetic comedy as well. If you ever actually watch Andrew playing it's always this pained, wide-mouthed expression from the moment the track starts to the end. Very funny.

In the four years spent in and out of Morrissey's company as his loyal traps player, I can now say with complete honesty that it was chock full of some of the finest moments of my musical life and inspired me to do anything else but earn a living exclusively from drumming. My rather limited view of the world was expanded by the experience sufficiently to realise that I had now the confidence to do something other than explain to people why I didn't look like a drummer, even though I was.

It's important to remember that Morrissey was and remains the great abstainer, so tea and the odd beer is about as rock 'n' roll as it gets. He is his own universe and as long as you bring your own oxygen, you'll have a great time.

Picture Credits

All images are courtesy of the interviewee excepting:

Manuel Cuevas © Cambridge Jones
Annie Ross © The David Beyda Studio, NYC
Ann Behringer © Buzz Harris
Andrew McGibbon © Simon Rix